THE DILIGENCE FIX

THE DILIGENCE FIX

How Striving for More Revenue Stresses Your Sales Organization and What to Do about It

Dayna Williams

ISBN: 979-8-9864846-0-0 (paperback)

— = notes in this chapter

Table of Contents

Preface

One particular bright spot over the past five years of my life was my opportunity to serve as a contributor to the Association for Talent Development, a prominent organization that supports the many facets of the talent development profession. My work ranged from writing for their print magazine or website and supporting the sales enablement community of practice as programming chair for their annual conference. Since its inception, the event has been branded as SELL (Sales Enablement Learning and Leadership), with a focus on bringing together professional education for industry practitioners. The speakers were invited based on their working knowledge of relevant topics such as training, coaching, onboarding, manager enablement, and the like.

Whether designing the programming strategy for SELL or reflecting back on my eighteen years of working with sales organizations, I have always been intrigued by how those topics and other sales development realities will transcend industry, size, and maturation. Inherent within the business of *any* business, regardless of specific circumstance and nuance, within our companies there's this shared sense of responsibility for sales and revenue. If you are reading this book, chances are you shoulder some portion of that responsibility—and if you are like many of the wonderful people I've met throughout the years who chose this profession, you personally own the commitment you've made to advance the strategy within your organization. Thank you for that leadership.

A few years ago, I was on a rather spirited call with a group of experienced sales enablement leaders. These individuals were in the final lap of preparing to present at the upcoming SELL conference. As the discussion was winding down, the group touched on some of the development issues that were top of mind for that quarter. Here are a few of the highlights from our informal chatter:

- We launched our sales process last year, but the sales team is still doing their own thing.
- Earlier this year, we brought all our managers together for a two-day coaching class, but we're not seeing much traction—they are still telling salespeople what to do.
- Our company made a huge investment in a new platform to give the sales team deeper insights, but we haven't been able to get the full-scale adoption that we wanted.
- My sellers are really good people, and they've been with us for a long time. During our sales kickoff, we brought in a sales trainer to work with them on questioning skills, but transactional selling continues to be their comfort zone.

I'm curious—can you relate to this list? For my part, the impromptu back and forth was interesting to observe. Sometimes the richest dialogue whips up rather spontaneously!

This banter continued for several more minutes. Then someone from the group invited my input: "Dayna, what do you think?"

I paused for a few seconds and then shared my honest feedback: "It sounds like a consistency issue." While these sales enablement practitioners were working on different initiatives, I couldn't help but notice a common thread running through each one—behavioral inconsistency. Each example suggested a strong start to the work effort, but as time passed, issues with maintaining traction began to emerge.

Fast-forward a few years, and with more research and insight into the underlying root cause, if they asked me again, I'd modify the response I gave. If we were to play back that same group conversation today and run down the challenges that they were working through, I would offer this revised feedback: *It sounds like a diligence issue.*

Diligence is both a matter of methodical, excellent work and a matter of character. Its various dimensions can become a template for individual behavior and can be operationalized within the business to drive the best results. When diligence blooms, you see consistent outputs like persuasion, grit, resilience, accountability, and more. In the pages that follow, we will explore diligence from both a philosophical perspective and as a set of salesperson capabilities that influence their behavior. When diligence is woven into the fabric of your organization, it introduces a standard that chips away at inconsistent behavior and its consequences on the business.

Together we will look at diligence within the context of a scientifically validated framework that underwrites the way you lead the team, develop your salespeople, and execute on your sales plan. For companies in growth mode, diligence is also the gateway to attracting the right talent while deeply motivating your existing team. Comprised of two distinctive elements—core selling and personal leadership qualities—diligence can become your blueprint for building next-level capabilities within your salespeople. This combination of both sales *and* personal leadership will position sellers to win more with clients now and increase their value as professionals by preparing them for the next level of career success. When this happens, you have the added bonus of amassing a pipeline of internal candidates who are equipped to become leadership successors within the sales function or more broadly throughout the company.

Imagine the possibilities if, in addition to driving revenue, part of your sales organization's internal brand was its ability to select, grow, and export the best talent within the company. That recognition is within your reach.

Introduction

A great change sits on the horizon. Just fifteen years ago, we thought the internet and the speed at which we were now able to access information, comparison shop, and connect with others was enough evolution to last us for a lifetime. But now a new reality bears down on us. Artificial intelligence (AI) has stealthily moved from the pages of science fiction to the workplace. As of this writing, companies that are integrating this technology into their business are still the exception—but not for long. We are in the predawn hours of a widespread intelligence revolution. So how ready are we?

If the COVID-19 phenomenon taught us anything, it was an object lesson in how unprepared we were for handling a massive disruption in life and in business. Literally overnight many companies had to convert their operations from office-based formats into more of a distributed work model. Most lacked the norms, systems, processes, and policies to support this seismic shift. Managers had to learn how to lead virtual teams without the comfort and reliability of face-to-face interactions. Likewise, many individual contributors found their resilience tested as they learned to cope in an isolated environment, lacking collaboration and experiencing some serious Zoom burnout. After a while, there arose this dueling sense of craving the return to normalcy while recognizing that the pandemic has, for better or worse, left its thumbprint on our work forever.

If the onset of a relatively transient virus had this kind of lasting impact on our work, it's not hard to imagine what's potentially in store as the barriers to entry with AI get lower and as acquiring this technology becomes more practical. In the race to stay competitive, growth-oriented companies will make increasingly greater investment in targeted AI solutions that promise to save time, bring actionable insights, automate tasks, increase accuracy, and guide outcomes leading to greater return on investment. It is easy to see how this sort of advantage could get addicting quickly. You could almost see acquiring more AI-powered solutions as an arms race of sorts between competitive companies or within certain industry segments. Even reluctant adopters will be forced to catch up quickly or risk becoming like the many retailers who dug in their heels, refused the mandate for change, and suffered the consequences.

As AI becomes more integrated into the everyday life of business, the sales profession, like many others, is destined for a massive disruption. Of course, some things will get easier. Salespeople will be able to rely on machines to guide them on which clients to pursue or which solutions or pricing formulas will work best given all the different variables. However, this also means that the role of the salesperson will become much more specialized. As this happens, they will need to master a hybrid dynamic that includes human and machine intelligence working together to drive revenue and other critical outcomes. As clients adopt AI on their side, they will demand more from their salesperson interactions—more data, comparative insights, and quantifiable recommendations. They will want this information faster, and they will expect the salesperson to package up this detail and deliver precise recommendations.

Research by Sirius Decisions estimates that today, 67 percent of the buyer's journey now happens digitally.[1] No doubt this will only

1 Matthew Parker, "67% of the Buyer's Journey Is Now Done Digitally—3 Ways to Deal with This," Profitable Print Relationships, accessed June 18, 2022, https://profitableprintrelationships.com/67-of-the-buyers-journey-is-now-done-digitally-3-ways-to-deal-with-this.

increase as we see AI gain more prominence in sales and marketing to help inform the prospective buyer well before they ever engage with a salesperson. This means that salespeople will need to be able to seamlessly take the baton from marketing and demonstrate mastery within an accelerated, data-driven digital sales environment.

Before we get too caught up in the future, we have to address where most sales organizations are today in their own evolution. Salespeople are not ready to thrive in this intelligence revolution. In fact, year after year, sales leaders find themselves revisiting the basics over and over again with their teams to try to form good solution selling habits, often with mixed outcomes. A quick glance at a few statistics paints the picture:

- Business-to-business (B2B) buyers report that fewer than one out of three salespeople can hold an effective conversation with senior executives.[2]
- Executive buyers believe that only 20 percent of the salespeople they meet with are successful in achieving their expectations and creating value. Only one in four get agreement from these buyers to meet again.[3]
- As many as 90 percent of buyers would meet with sellers earlier but are delaying these conversations because they believe that sellers don't take the time to understand their business and add value.[4]

---

2 Steve W. Martin, "7 Reasons Salespeople Don't Close the Deal," Harvard Business Review, August 2, 2017, https://hbr.org/2017/08/7-reasons-salespeople-dont-close-the-deal.

3 Mark Lindwall, "Why Don't Buyers Want to Meet with Your Salespeople?," Forrester, September 29, 2014, www.forrester.com/blogs/14-09-29-why_dont_buyers_want_to_meet_with_your_salespeople.

4 CSO Insights, "The Growing Buyer-Seller Gap: Results of the 2018 Buyer Preference Study," 2018, https://pleinairestrategies.com/wp-content/uploads/2018/09/CSO-Growing-Buyer-Seller-Gap-White-paper_FINAL-1.pdf.

- Of the executive buyers surveyed on their meetings with salespeople, 70 percent report that sellers are not prepared for the questions they ask, and 77 percent don't think that sellers understand the issues they deal with and where to help.[5]

This is the current state for many organizations. So if we woke up tomorrow and mass implementation of AI was the new normal in the same way that COVID-19 roared onto the scene, most teams would get caught utterly flat-footed and underprepared.

We aren't there yet, but we can't sit back either. The greatest opportunity many sales leaders have right now is to prepare their teams for increased growth as the market continues to rebound. It means leading a complete top-down maturation of the sales function. In other words, taking steps to formalize total alignment among communicating the sales vision, activating managers-as-coaches, developing salesperson capability, and fine-tuning processes across the board. In the pages that follow, I will refer to this alignment effort as a Sales Effectiveness Program and focus on how to systematically implement it.

In the aftermath of the pandemic, we'll have a brief window of time before the next disruption hits home. AI is coming, and for better or worse or both, it will bring with it a tidal wave of change. It will be important to lead from the front on this, to lay the groundwork within your organization and build capability in salespeople that will ensure that they are resilient and equipped for success in a brand-new reality. Sales leaders who take these steps now will enjoy the early advantages that come only from being proactive and prepared.

5 Mark Lindwall, "Why Don't Buyers Want to Meet with Your Salespeople?"

Part 1

Confronting Inconsistency

Chapter 1

Growth Breaks Things

Companies in growth mode have to relentlessly drive revenue quarter after quarter. The responsibility for ensuring that happens largely falls at the feet of sales leadership. Whether this charge is handed to a CEO within an early-stage growth company or a head of sales in a midsize company, leading this function is unquestionably one of the most challenging positions in business. Of course, if you are one of those team members who works tirelessly in a supporting management or sales operations role, chances are you too feel the pressure to perform. A company's very existence will rise and fall on its sales performance.

Sales leaders are responsible for synthesizing marketplace realities with company capabilities, fostering lead generation efforts, executing on a plan to meet revenue expectations, and managing through any number of internal constraints. For companies in aggressive growth mode, a sales leader's work is largely focused on rapidly addressing performance gaps and fine-tuning their approaches to keep pace. These leaders often need to drive results through their existing sales teams, which may be a mixed bag of talent and abilities. When performance falls short, sales leaders must quickly appraise the situation, adapt, and take action to effectively course correct.

CRACKS AND QUICK FIXES

The pace at which most sales leaders have to work today to remain market competitive is both understandable and problematic at the same time. Without realizing it, things can get myopic quickly. It is easy to become too focused on the daily grind—those everyday activities of running a sales practice—and lose sight of the big picture. This is also commonly known as working in the business.

Oftentimes, when the pressure is on to drive revenue and the work pace is accelerated, things can break. The demand for more productivity is always a reliable stress test for your people, process, and platforms. When cracks begin to appear, the temptation to reach for quick fixes is real. Anything that promises to address the inconsistencies that start to set in when driving for next-level growth seems attractive. Especially if you can throw money at a problem and have someone else take care of it for you—that seems like a best-case scenario!

Perhaps the quick fix looks like an outsourced sales training program to help your team get better at negotiating or handling objections. Or maybe it's a customer relationship management (CRM) enhancement to help salespeople get more regimented about how they prepare for calls. In either case, chances are the vendor made all sorts of assurances that these solutions were exactly what you needed to solve your challenges, so you purchased and ran with it.

Fast-forward a few months, and you think that your eyes are deceiving you—the same performance cracks that prompted you to go vendor shopping are starting to show again! That's because these proverbial Band-Aids don't work over the long haul. Instead, these quick fixes are like wallpapering over a gaping hole. If you don't address underlying structural issues in your sales operation, then all the one-off vendor solutions or internal special projects won't move the performance needle. In the worst-case scenarios, they can even confuse or frustrate the sales team.

The weight of being in growth mode can compromise the infrastructure you've built to date. In order to keep meeting higher and higher revenue targets, a sales operation—which was likely built to perform at a lower growth interval—will need to stretch and contort itself to pursue more clients and bring in more money. While this is going on, your team doesn't have enough bandwidth to work on the business and ensure that the team's operational chassis is strong and stable enough to support new demands. It's one thing to push hard to finish the first quarter strong. But if that same push happens in Q2 and Q3, the sales team is now officially operating on a different plane. If during this growth-driven evolution, reactive quick fixes were the only go-to answers for people, process, or platform issues, then those cracks are inevitable. These cracks start off looking like inconsistent behavior or performance, and with time they can worsen to a point of dysfunction and counterproductivity.

START WITH AN HONEST ANALYSIS

Most business leaders are good at noticing cracks. In fact, the more severe the cracks, the more likely they will get a lot of attention. Planning discussions around what upgrades are needed so that the sales team can keep pace with growth will undoubtedly ensue. The challenge is that these same leaders who are feverishly working in the business each day to devise strategy and drive performance are too close to the problems to be truly objective in solving them.

Before decisions are made around the right fixes, it is important to do some forensic work to uncover and analyze the origins of the performance-related and functional gaps. This important analysis begins with a review of four key areas within the sales organization:

1. Methodology and Process
2. Sales Development Strategy
3. Seller Performance (individually, team based)
4. Manager Effectiveness

For each area, determine the ideal state and business impact for each. Work through the list and ask the following questions:

- Does this area exist today in our organization?
- How formalized is it? Who owns it?
- In what ways is it aiding our sales strategy and growth efforts?
- Where are the gaps? Will this area be sufficient one to two years from now?
- Related to this area, do our people understand their role and why it matters to their work?

This legwork helps you see whether current less-than-ideal outcomes stem from something missing or broken at the sales function level, whether it is more about seller performance, or both. It provides a first glimpse into pockets of inconsistency that may be weakening the sales team's operational chassis. Armed with this insight, a sales leader can also determine what *is* working so that they can leverage it further.

Take, for instance, new hires and their ramp-up curve. If new salespeople are hitting targets within the first six months, and these new team members are crediting posthire training with giving them a solid knowledge base, then this is strong, confirming evidence. Your onboarding program (as part of your Sales

Development Strategy) is producing consistent results. It's a pillar that you can lean on to support future growth within the sales function.

Now let's consider for a moment that the opposite is true. Suppose the onboarding program is ineffective. Maybe the idea was for it to be manager led, but those managers have very full plates, and as a result, new salespeople are left to their own devices. Within the first six months, these individuals seem busy, but they are not producing. Taking a closer look, you realize that varying degrees of knowledge are in play. Sellers are fuzzy about your company's ideal prospect profile, product catalog, or pricing model. They lack the confidence and basic building blocks necessary to be successful. All signs point to a near-certain conclusion. The current approach to onboarding new salespeople is producing inconsistent results.

When left unchecked, inconsistency slowly but steadily works against your interest as a sales leader. When it infiltrates companies in aggressive growth mode, inconsistency is a progressively destabilizing force that eats away at your efforts to fine-tune the sales operation. Its constant presence and the fires it ignites are a personal energy drain. For every hard-won step forward, the consequences of inconsistency can push you five steps back.

INCONSISTENT BEHAVIOR

While inconsistency is inherent within human behavior and therefore may never be fully eradicated, it can be subdued and controlled. The potential benefits of tackling this subtle but effective growth killer makes it a worthwhile leadership pursuit. Consistently run sales organizations generate more predictable outcomes, reduce overall risk, and attract the best talent while increasing team morale.

The earliest indicators of inconsistency tend to reveal

themselves within the context of salesperson behavior. John isn't asking enough questions. Tamara doesn't use CRM the way she should. When seller behavior misses the mark, it is just so easy to observe. At first glance, it might look like inconsistent behavior stems from a few rogue individuals. However, it is almost always a symptom of larger problems within the sales function itself. These pesky behaviors are a mirror of sorts that reveals deeper issues.

For example, in B2B selling, we often emphasize the importance of salespeople being more relationship oriented with clients rather than being transactional. In other words, we want salespeople to be motivated by helping the client meet their objectives. This often means that the salesperson needs to be working toward cultivating a longer-term commitment with their client, as opposed to just closing a deal—*any* deal.

Despite manager coaching on this topic, let's say that you have a sales team that is still focused on winning deals and then quickly moving on to other opportunities. They aren't taking the time to forge relationships with their client contacts. This could be a comfort zone thing. Or it could be that salespeople are picking up on some mixed internal messages. On the one hand, they hear that relationship building is important, but on the other hand, the only thing that seems to truly matter is quota. They aren't sure what they will win if they focus on relationships, but it *is* clear what they'll lose if they don't meet their quarterly goal. In the prior scenario, the sales team's behavior, specifically their lack of consistent effort to build client relationships, may be a symptom of a common root issue: mixed internal messaging about what matters most to the company.

Mixed messaging happens when two dueling topics compete for prominence with each other. One topic involves the methods and behaviors that sales leaders want to see their teams put into action. The other relates to sales goals. While methods and behavior will get some planned and spontaneous attention (especially when someone makes an error), messaging around sales goals often wins the top spot.

This is, of course, because results matter. Sales leaders also spend a great deal of their own time on goal planning, forecasting, and reporting. This includes reverse engineering annual revenue expectations, carving it up, and assigning it across the sales team. This work is nearly always top of mind for sales leaders, so it's easy to hyperfocus on it with the team. However, when the sales planning approach and subsequent messaging to salespeople becomes all about tactics and goals, it tends to take on the characteristics of a duck hunt—territory, targets, and tracking.

After leaders share this tactical plan with the sales team, the three Ts often become the subject of an endless conversation loop. Every manager check-in, every communication, is about pipeline, CRM, documentation, reporting, and the like. Each quarterly update is focused on—you guessed it—territory, targets, and tracking. When this happens, salespeople will take you literally—the three Ts are all that matter here. Even if you communicate these metrics with some additional guidance or direction, the majority of your team will still conclude that it's really just about the three Ts.

SALESPEOPLE ARE CHAMELEONS

When salespeople see that territory, targets, and tracking are the exclusive focus, heavily reinforced within the workflow, they'll adjust their tactics accordingly. Although these elements are important, when the focus is too narrow, it leaves things like methods or approaches up to individual interpretation. When sales leaders are messaging three to one in favor of the three Ts, salespeople start drawing their own conclusions about what it means to sell at your organization. This can be ground zero for widespread behavioral inconsistency.

Salespeople don't just take their cues from your messaging. They also observe the accepted behavior around them. Most salespeople have this wonderful, chameleon-style quality of becoming like the environment they are in. When they deploy this ability with clients, it tends to serve them well. Clients are likely to perceive these malleable qualities as relatable or personable. However, salespeople will bring this same quality into their workplaces. They will look for clues about what actions are allowable within their sales organization. While salespeople may hear your messaging around expectations, they will also compare that with what they see others do and whether that behavior gets acknowledged, recognized, ignored, or swept under the carpet. Then they will act in the way that most serves their interests, so long as it is either rewarded or allowed to continue without consequence. Consider this candid and important truth: *Salespeople will almost always discount spoken standards if they see contrary actions being rewarded or tolerated.* If they hear you say that sales process is important, but the top performer on the team has a reputation for skirting that process and still gets applauded, the takeaway is that making your numbers is the only thing that matters. The more frequent these sorts of disconnects are allowed to persist within a sales organization, the more likely salespeople will adopt a by-any-means-necessary mindset. When this happens, salespeople slowly become their own arbitrators of what behaviors or actions are necessary to drive activity and meet their goals. This reality is compounded when sales managers overlook or excuse bad behavior because it's connected to winning a big deal.

Of course, flexibilities may be necessary to produce short-term wins. The difference is that if your sales organization has a by-any-means-necessary current running throughout, a long-term cost is accruing. Think about it as a steady drip of fuel for inconsistency. The more chronic inconsistency becomes over time, the more it seeps into your system and can become completely unmanageable.

INCONSISTENCY WITHIN THE SALES FUNCTION

Inconsistent behavior is one type of headache. However, when the problem becomes more systemic, as it begins to infect the sales function, it can be harder to fully assess what's going on. Such attempts are like a murky expedition to the bottom of a steep riverbed—you just never know what you're going to find as you continue the descent. For that reason, it may be tempting to skip the dive altogether. Sometimes it just seems safer to press on with the tactics of territory, targets, and tracking, leaving matters of inconsistency unaddressed for the moment. Of course, time has a way of stratifying these issues, which only makes the potential consequences that much more severe.

Consider the plight of one particular business leader with a sales organization of about thirty-five people. Focused on ambitious growth, the company looked the other way as each salesperson did their own thing within their territories. They ganged up on any attempts to standardize process or approach, and each time leadership didn't push the issue. However, when it came time to accelerate a new go-to-market plan by migrating the team to Salesforce, it took months of costly consulting and analysis to piece together a common Sales Process that was supportive of the company's sales strategy and could be used to customize the platform. Efforts to then train the sales team as well as other business partners required not only teaching the CRM but also the newly standardized Sales Process—which was now a nonnegotiable. On top of that, leadership introduced about a half dozen new presales and post-sales processes at the same time that were necessary to support this more formalized approach. After the training and socialization efforts, team productivity ground to a halt. The shock of having to introduce too much too fast left this sales team drowning in a confusing sea of process and standardization. Most found it nearly impossible to take even the smallest steps forward.

While this example highlights extreme issues with anything-goes salesperson behavior, it is easy to see how the issues also connect back to gaps in the sales function. Failure to keep pace with business growth and get ahead of opportunities to formalize things creates systemic inconsistency. Every sales organization has its tipping point, and for this particular company, it was the implementation of Salesforce and all that went with it. In their slow but steady march to CRM migration, leadership faced many decision points along the way. They could have confronted consistency issues one-by-one before everything combined for an ill-timed avalanche. The lesson here is straightforward: the presence of inconsistency in any sales organization offers a choice—a leadership decision to confront the issues or punt until a later day.

The previous example primarily illustrates how inconsistent process is a common gap within companies that are growing quickly. However, there are other ways that inconsistency shows up within a business. These include the following:

- The company's value proposition is weak without enough perceived value.
- The go-to-market plan is not aligned to market needs or to the capabilities of the business.
- The sales team composition (roles, staffing levels, organization, manager-to-seller ratio) is not sufficient to support executing on the sales plan.

- The sales team does not understand or chooses not to execute the sales plan; they either don't meet role expectations or their performance isn't aligned with how they will be measured or compensated.
- At the start of a new year, the organization may be in between sales plans and is sending mixed messages to the sales team to follow the former plan while openly speculating about changes due to take place within the new plan.
- There is no defined Sales Process (what you do), stages, key activities, evidentiary outcomes, or Methodology (how you do it) to create shared language and understanding among the team.
- There are no enforced standards around proper deal documentation within the CRM or expectations around strong internal handoffs.
- Technology infrastructure does not support the needs of the sales team (it may be old, outdated, not customized, underutilized, or misused).
- A product or service offering and its corresponding pricing structure is underdefined, allowing room for the sales team to improvise and potentially resulting in lower margin deals.
- Sales managers were promoted from being individual contributors without any prior experience leading people.
- Sales managers struggle to effectively coach and develop sellers, especially those who are different from them.
- Sales training efforts are not connected to a strategic development plan, and thus actual results from these fragmented offerings become difficult to track.
- Salesperson recruiting efforts lack objective data and insight to determine whether the candidate's personality

traits and prior experience will translate to success at their new organization.

- New seller onboarding is a firehose of information, lacking real-world context and structured on-the-job practice to accelerate effectiveness.
- The sales team culture is loosely defined and inconsistently holds people accountable for activity and behavior.

It might be helpful to read over this list a few times and to consider highlighting the issues that could have an impact in your organization. Is it possible that a few of these might make for some good conversation starters at one of your management meetings?

ILLUSTRATING CONSISTENCY

Next, let's look at the potential impact when these issues are in play. For illustrative purposes, we'll descend upon a fictitious sales organization that is experiencing some growth pains, including having missed revenue targets the last two quarters. Assume for a few moments that you have a bird's-eye view of the happenings within this business. From this high perch, you can observe a few drivers of inconsistency at work and draw some of your own conclusions about the potential consequences.

The first thing you notice is the way this company's sales team is set up. It doesn't look like it is adequate enough to support the needs of its approved go-to-market plan. The job description for its B2B sellers requires a mix of both hunting and farming skills to originate and close deals. Yet the current sales team roster is full of farmers. They don't have the skills or the confidence to successfully hunt for new logos.

As a result, these sellers gravitate to lower-hanging deals—the kind that will close easily. Of course, there aren't enough of those turnkey deals to meet their goals, and so as the pressure to perform mounts, it creates some undesirable outcomes. As soon as these salespeople get in front of new clients, they turn into order-takers. Their skill set isn't strong enough to confidently lead a consultative sale, and so many of the deals they write up are outside of the company's core capabilities. Yet for the sake of quota, their manager pushes them through, creating all sorts of downstream headaches. Having the wrong people in the wrong seats on this sales team means fewer new clients and lower deal quality from existing clients.

Adding to the ability gap, this sales team is also shorthanded. They are down two full-time salespeople, and this open head-count means that at least 20 percent of new leads and existing accounts aren't being covered. To make matters worse, you notice that the company is recruiting sales candidates using the same hunting-and-farming job description. If they bring on two ill-fitting new team members, the talent gap is poised to widen, and the cycle of inadequate performance will surely repeat itself.

Next, you observe the company's sales managers. This group was primarily promoted from within and were formerly individual contributors. Now as managers of people, they have a stubborn habit of telling their sellers what to do. They take a one-size-fits-all approach to these conversations, which drains a lot of time from their day. Instead of these salespeople getting better at solving their challenges, they are becoming more dependent on their sales managers' direction. Despite the time and effort, performance remains mediocre.

Taking a closer look at what development options are available to close some of these performance gaps, you notice that the company offers a large catalog of sales training courses through their learning management system (LMS). Two on-site workshops occur each year. At the annual kickoff, leadership always makes a point to include a fairly engaging skill-building session. At first glance, this blended approach seems to check all the training boxes well enough. But when you see how it plays out from a higher vantage point, the development plan seems rather ad hoc, almost disjointed.

To a salesperson, this training approach might feel almost like binge-watching a series on Netflix or Hulu. While they're immersed in the content, there's an interesting and possibly even an entertaining quality to it. However, after the last episode, chances are the viewer removes the title from their watchlist and shifts their attention to whatever's next. The downside of content overload is that it has become the norm to passively consume information without any responsibility to do something with it. You can see how the same may be true with episodic, disjointed sales training. As the sales team consumes the content, there may be a moment or two of relevance, but if it's not connected to a broader plan that addresses the big gaps you're seeing, it's doubtful that there will be any real change.

This hypothetical exercise teases out three common causes of inconsistency within the sales function and how these issues play out in real time:

1. The wrong sales team composition
2. Underdeveloped managers
3. Unaddressed salesperson skill gaps

Of course, this same fictional company could have just as easily had more like five or eight issues simmering and compounding beneath the surface, all working against growth efforts.

As with any journey, awareness is the first step, so let's start with this truth: Inconsistency is an indisputable progress killer. Now for some good news. There is a way to correct these imbalances and gradually fortify your organization so that it's well positioned to support the continued growth of your business. The answer is getting serious about implementing a Sales Effectiveness Program within your organization. This approach is about creating total alignment from strategy through implementation and evaluation that begins to chip away at inconsistency. The Sales Effectiveness Program is anchored by a fortifying framework and spans the three critical elements of Methodology, Process, and Development to help move the sales team, and the organization, forward.

As a leader weighing this prospective challenge, perhaps you're feeling an internal fire starting to ignite. The choice to confront and tackle inconsistency is bold, but it's also one of the most important investments you can make. In so doing, you can bank on a spectacular payoff in more ways than one.

Chapter 2

A Fortifying Framework

Whether the origins of inconsistency lie within the behavior of our salespeople or whether it lurks within the corners of our sales function, we've explored how it can keep our important initiatives from gaining traction and stymie growth efforts.

Confronting this problem begins anchoring your sales organization to a broader framework. There simply has to be an overarching umbrella—a North Star of sorts that drives consistency by guiding behaviors and actions. Something directional beyond just territories, targets, and tracking that helps the sales organization's tires grip the roadway. The idea is that this fortifying framework will underwrite the various components of the organization's new Sales Effectiveness Program. In time, this program becomes the blueprint for how work gets done, why technology or tools are rolled out, and what we expect out of sellers.

Introducing a fortifying framework as a first step on the journey toward sales effectiveness might feel like a culture play, and to some degree it is. However, simply adorning an office wall or website with a shiny set of core values or buzzwords won't suffice. Any framework worth organizing around must be inherently practical. It must be fully implementable within a real-world sales team and have enough science, substance, and sustaining potential to actually impact the consistency issue—both behaviorally and within the sales function itself.

The Diligence Framework fits that bill. Its content flows from some of the top literature in the sales field today and is comprised of ten well-researched dimensions. Most importantly, it has been shaped and pressure-tested according to what it takes for salespeople to successfully perform in today's complex environment. As a set of well-defined principles and capabilities, this modern framework is a well-suited candidate for becoming that overarching umbrella for growth-minded sales leaders who want to preside over more consistent organizations.

DUE DILIGENCE OR DO DILIGENCE

As we get started, it may be helpful to explore the question, Why diligence? For many leaders, this term is most recognizable within the context of due diligence. In routine business matters, this concept is often connected to financial practices or legal matters. It also comes into play before acquiring higher-priced assets such as real estate. Perhaps, though, the highest, most robust form of due diligence is associated with merger and acquisition (M&A) activity, which has almost become commonplace across the business landscape today.

Over the last decade, the combined impact of various geopolitical factors and macro trends in the US market produced a record spike in the buying, selling, and consolidating of businesses. Then came the year 2020. Suddenly we watched the world economy flip onto its backside. Any active M&A investors either camped on the sidelines or ventured into more of a salvage-like mission, focusing on different opportunities like restructures or bailouts. Regardless of market conditions or deal type, the discipline of due diligence remains an integral part of any M&A transaction. After all, there's serious money on the line.

If you've had any sort of view into this process, you know it is thorough, exacting, and at times ferocious. Due diligence is designed to produce a comprehensive view into the health and viability of a prospective asset. The stakes are high, and so those in charge take deep ownership over accuracy and outcomes. In fact, it is not uncommon to hear those involved in the process say something like, "We expect much greater clarity after our due diligence."

There is an implied confidence in what has become to some an almost sacred practice. Due diligence is like a three-sided prism. It is an expectation, an event, and a process all rolled into one neon phrase. It carries weight and is reserved mostly for high-stakes scenarios. For leaders and key team members tasked with playing a role in due diligence, it becomes one of their greatest priorities. These people double- or triple-check submissions and carefully guard against the risk of omitting any relevant information. At the heart of due diligence is a standard of care. It is a shared belief that ensuring our interests ahead of an impending case, purchase, or transaction is *so* critical that we are going to take a defined set of rigorous steps to do so.

DILIGENCE IS VERSATILE

Few would argue that revenue and sales are not mission-critical to the health and viability of growth-oriented companies. So if due diligence is reserved for only the most important, high-stakes business matters, what lessons can we take from that? Would our sales organization benefit from extracting some of that diligence DNA, sequencing it to our work, and infusing it throughout the function? Hint: yes!

When diligence as defined by the Diligence Framework is

practiced within a sales context, it becomes a predictable, stabilizing force. As it becomes the sales organization's North Star, running like a red thread throughout the function, the message is clear. Revenue is so important to our organization that we cannot take chances. We simply cannot risk our people being underdeveloped to perform strategically and consistently with our clients. We cannot divert valuable management resources toward cleaning up the remnants of bad seller behavior, nor can we allow its consequences to stress our internal systems. We also cannot afford not knowing or ignoring quiet leaks in our process that place client opportunities at risk.

If adopted, Diligence and its spectrum of principles, capabilities, behaviors, and actions can be a game changer for your sales organization. Together, we'll unpack the Diligence Framework and thoroughly define its components in the pages that follow. Finally, we'll cover a phased plan to implement the Diligence Framework and the various elements of the Sales Effectiveness Program within your sales function.

Table 1. Ten Dimensions of Diligence

Selling Dimensions	**Personal Leadership Dimensions**
• Growing Relationships • Situational Intelligence • Securing Information • Intentional Listening • Persuasive Communication	• Personal Ownership • Time Planning • Service Mindset • Winning Drive • Inner Resolve

This framework can be woven throughout your sales organization and applied flexibly to drive the right outcomes. First and foremost, the ten Diligence Dimensions should be applied as salesperson *competencies*, because in their purest form, they define ideal seller behaviors. Competencies are a staple of organizational behavior work. They help leaders objectively define the right knowledge, skills, and abilities needed for success. Competencies can also bring clarity to the hiring process.

The Diligence Dimensions present the ten most important competencies for high performance in a B2B sales environment, where it is important to cultivate new relationships and expand existing ones. When these dimensions-as-competencies are practiced with consistency and mastery, salespeople will perform at upper-intermediate and advanced levels. For newer or underperforming salespeople, these competencies can serve as a benchmark to establish where they are now and what areas they need to develop in order to perform consistently well.

FRINGE GAPS

There are a lot of good competency libraries out there. The challenge for growth organizations is that most sales competencies focus on the basic blocking and tackling of selling skills and abilities at the individual contributor level. That may serve your developmental interests to a point, but those cracks that come with accelerated growth aren't solved by just focusing on the basics of selling. The more your team has to adjust to the demands of higher productivity, the more likely new and more complex behavioral issues will emerge. Chances are those basic competencies aren't nuanced enough to help you diagnose these new problems. Nor do they help you identify the more subtle gaps that tend to occur around the fringes of the work stream, those gray areas where balls can drop.

Take, for instance, the basic salesperson competency of Gathering Information. This is a staple, in some form or another, within most existing sales frameworks. Conventional thinking and years of consultative selling wisdom have emphasized the great importance of asking questions and uncovering client needs during the sales process. So a Gathering Information competency essentially exists to help measure the important skill of discovery in salespeople.

Of course, even if every salesperson on your team nailed the art of discovery, there would still be evidence of behavioral inconsistency—primarily around the fringes or the seams of that process. As an example, what good is discovery if a salesperson cannot filter through the information they've uncovered, make sense of it, document it, and retrieve it for use later down the line in the sales process? In other words, if we focus on just the competency of Gathering Information and put salespeople through several iterations of training around questioning skills, and if we coach them on being curious to understand client needs, but they don't follow through on the other work stream responsibilities to store and safeguard that client information, the end result will still be fraught with consistency issues.

As more and more salespeople keep contributing to these fringe gaps, the more these undesirable outcomes start compounding across the team. Soon this matter of inconsistency becomes systemic. You start talking with your sales operations team about why reporting isn't accurate and why CRM isn't the wealth of client intelligence that it should be. Of course, the best outputs are always dependent on the right inputs.

The Diligence dimensions-as-competencies provide more coverage over these sorts of fringe gaps. Its more inclusive design gives traditional competencies like Gathering Information a modern-day makeover. Within the Diligence Framework, you won't find Gathering Information in the traditional sense. Instead, we call it Securing Information. While the Securing Information competency includes the same core elements of Gathering Information, namely its focus on discovery skills, it also introduces new color and nuance by including related (but often overlooked) behaviors like the following:

- Utilizing a set of practical standards to determine the quality and relevance of information
- Capturing, organizing, and documenting information for easy access and retrieval

Securing Information goes beyond Gathering Information by placing an added emphasis on the capture of quality and relevant information (implying the need for a method to determine quality and relevance over general intake). It also introduces an element around the safeguarding and retrieval of client information. This is important because salespeople often don't document well. This is a prime example of a common fringe gap that causes plenty of downstream headaches. Handoffs can break down, and ultimately the client experience may not be what it should be. Because these sorts of fringe gaps are rarely measured, they often don't get monitored or managed either. But yet this sales behavior (or lack thereof) actually matters! As the volume of sales activity increases to meet growth demands, being able to capture and retain more client details from each interaction will provide a valuable information advantage. Diligence dimensions-as-competencies provide this sort of coverage for fringe gaps across the selling spectrum. Sales leaders can use these competencies to address the basic blocking and tackling of selling while also chipping away at those previously undetected peripheral behaviors and fringe gaps. They are used best as an objective means to define, measure, and ultimately remediate salesperson behavior challenges before they become systemic.

PERSONAL LEADERSHIP DIFFERENTIATOR

The Diligence Framework complements its five core selling competencies with five personal leadership competencies to create a unique developmental mash-up. This combination is rarely introduced at the individual seller level. More typically, these leadership competencies show up at the manager level. However, as growth demands a higher level of performance, it is critical to develop salespeople who can maintain a strategic view of their opportunities and accounts while taking ownership over driving results.

The fact that most common sales frameworks stop short of effectively defining and measuring the personal leadership side of the developmental equation is a miss. Individual sellers who are skilled at their craft and have a strong personal leadership foundation represent the ultimate versatility player. They can be deployed on strategic, complex deals. They can also serve as informal player-coaches to their peers.

In addition, these individuals can operate in an advisory role to you as a sales leader and aid in problem-solving or idea generation. They will not only be great sellers but also become levers of consistency within your organization. The more visibility and influence they have, and the more they are recognized for their consistent behavior, the more others will follow. This creates a powerful multiplier effect that aids your leadership efforts to instill consistency throughout the sales organization. At the very least, the momentum of stable salesperson behavior is surging in the right direction instead of working against you.

SERVING THE SALES FUNCTION

While we've covered the importance of competencies to define seller behavior, the Diligence Framework is also a means to strengthen the sales function. The ten Diligence Dimensions can act as a guiding hand, lending a set of beliefs and principles that the entire sales team can rally around. As you implement and reinforce principles like Personal Ownership or Time Planning or Situational Intelligence alongside the territory, targets, and tracking of your sales plan, you set new expectations around consistency for how the work gets done. When you recognize positive examples of these beliefs in action, it connects your people to something bigger. Specific to Personal Ownership, the more it shows up in how people work, the more of an antidote you have against the travails of inconsistency. Over time, individual behaviors and opinions are held to a higher standard, and an anything-goes environment gives way to one that is more predictable and process driven.

SUPPORTING DILIGENCE BEHAVIOR

As salespeople begin recognizing that their behavior must come into alignment with the diligence-driven competencies, the sales environment they work in must reinforce their development.

For instance, if salespeople need to plan their time well (Time Planning), and their calendars are bogged down with internal meetings, they should have enough latitude to decline certain meetings for the right reasons. They need to be encouraged to think and act like that. However, if the opposite is true and Time Planning efforts are met with blowback, then we're back at mixed messaging and all the challenges that can present. As a sales leader, your role is critical in driving that sort of top-down alignment until the Diligence beliefs and principles invade each nook and cranny of the sales organization.

As we further explore each Diligence Dimension, keep in mind the versatility of its application to both salesperson behavior and your sales function. Consider how implementing this fortifying framework in phases can create a common language, shared expectations, and an objective way to make decisions. Finally, think about how these dimensions enhance your territory, targets, and tracking efforts and enable the overall success of your sales plan.

Part 2

Developing Diligence – The Ten Dimensions

Chapter 3

Growing Relationships

Recognizes the value of consistently strong interactions with others as critical for building professional momentum, putting sustained, thoughtful effort into relationship-building actions that deepen trust and create win-win outcomes.

Choosing to begin with *Growing Relationships* as the first Diligence Dimension is purposeful, given how important relationships are to our work. In B2B selling, sometimes your only advantage over a competitor is to be the person your client wants to do business with. Internally, strong relationships among colleagues means establishing the most productive working conditions. When there is a mutual appreciation, people desire to work together and cocreate the best outcomes.

Growing Relationships goes far beyond likability and rapport—there is a strategy and method behind it. For instance, we might train salespeople on having strong interpersonal conversations, but what if they're spending their time engaging with the wrong account—the one with the thinnest, least likely opportunity to grow revenue? I intentionally use the word *Grow* instead of its familiar close cousins *Relationship Management* or *Relationship Building*, which are often found in other competency models. This is important because the broader focus covers some of those fringe gaps we mentioned previously, those aspects of a salesperson's work that can fall through the cracks.

At a quick first glance, Relationship Management seems to aptly describe what we want most salespeople to do. However, the problem with a management mindset is that it assumes the salesperson has enough control over the relationship and is therefore in a position to manage (or manipulate or maneuver) the client. How often is that the case? Not often, especially not early on in a relationship with a given client. So if you can't manage what you don't exercise enough control over, then perhaps that's where Building Relationships could be a focus. At least the concept of building implies a partnership between the salesperson and the client, though building is not an infinite endeavor. There's an implied end point to building. At some point, whether it involves building a structure or any other planned endeavor, the act of building draws to a close. Do we then want salespeople on cruise control within their seemingly established relationships? No. In contrast, we really want salespeople thinking about their relationships in the most collaborative, expansive terms.

Client relationships should have a renewable component to them. We want our salespeople in growth mode, which is why the more precise concept of Growing Relationships communicates the mindset and behavior that you want to see on display. Even if there is a finiteness to the nature of your business or sales cycle, established, sustainable relationships keep growing through referrals or positive word of mouth. Of course, the gold standard of growth is when a client contact moves to a new company and takes you with them. When that happens, it is by far the most observable reward of dogged, behind-the-scenes salesperson diligence. For these reasons, developing your salespeople toward Growing Relationships will surely cover components of building and managing while also going further to encourage the right actions and behaviors over time to maximize the full potential of your client accounts.

THREE WATCHOUTS

1. Taking a one-size-fits-all approach to early client outreaches
2. Prioritizing relationships based on personal likability, shared social interest, or level of comfort
3. Allowing large time gaps to occur after the win before reconnecting with the client

Ahead of discussing a series of beliefs that drive excellence in Growing Relationships, let's take a look at a few things that can get in the way. Watchouts are most commonly an awareness issue. A salesperson may not recognize their own habits or behaviors that actively work against their interests. Of course, some watchouts operate in the light of day. In these cases, both the sales manager and the seller are aware of negative tendencies or behavioral patterns, yet they aren't effectively addressing them in training or coaching.

Before we jump into watchouts that hinder efforts to Grow Relationships, let's take in these watchouts with a healthy balance of awareness, contemplation, and levity. It never hurts to nod and chuckle a bit as you begin to recognize certain things that get in the way.

First up, one of the great watchouts that hinders relationship growth is *taking a one-size-fits-all approach to early client outreaches.* A salesperson might justify replicating the outreach techniques they've seen work in the past. They may even suggest that this turnkey approach to business development is more efficient and that they are able to do more with less time. For argument's sake, let's assume that using the same techniques over and over again *can* net some results. What happens when, at a certain point, that's no longer true? What about those clients who have a need, but the script isn't resonating? Or perhaps the client doesn't fully recognize their needs yet, and so they tune the seller out.

The fix for this trouble spot is helping salespeople realize the balance. Efficiency is important, but they will go further faster with at least some modest tailoring to set the right tone with prospective clients. Yes, it takes more effort to quickly develop understanding and then filter things like your company or product value proposition through that lens. However, these small efforts help a salesperson gain traction quicker, and it sets them apart from all the other mediocre or annoying outreaches that prospective clients have come to expect. Part of averting this watchout is coaching, but the large portion rests with the salesperson, who has to put the added effort in when no one is watching.

Another watchout is the strong tendency toward *prioritizing relationships based on personal likability, shared social interest, or level of comfort.* In working with salespeople for many years, particularly testing out material within the classroom, I noticed that there's always at least one salesperson who is marginally flamboyant and a tad too confident. Interestingly enough, leadership often considers them one of the more successful sellers. These individuals may be prone to wearing Hawaiian shirts, jazzy socks, or some other attention-grabbing garb. They are often a little too tan for the time of year and are quick to insert stories of how their clients revere them and how their golf game isn't where they'd like it to be—but really, who's keeping score when the cart is stocked with everyone's favorite brews?

The point is, whether it's a Jazzy Jeff type or someone on

your team who is more down to earth, when salespeople prioritize their time with clients based off anything other than revenue and opportunity, this watchout is in play. Time is the salesperson's most limited nonrenewable resource. If a salesperson spends too much time with certain clients for reasons other than achieving strategic business goals, then this habit is a problem. Instead, we want to coach salespeople out of prioritizing their own preferences and into doing the harder work of objectively ranking their relationships according to revenue potential. Quite commonly, those relationships with the strongest growth potential may also be the most underdeveloped—thus requiring a heavier lift from the salesperson.

The final watchout happens post-sale. After sustained efforts to bring a deal over the line, sellers can falter by inadvertently *allowing large time gaps to occur after the win before reconnecting with the client.* This understandably occurs as salespeople go off to slay new dragons. The behavior may even seem appropriate after they made a solid handoff to, say, a post-sale implementation team. Regardless, from the client's perspective, the difference between all the attention that the salesperson lavished presale and the relatively low to no interaction post-sale is evident. This creates an unnecessary relationship risk.

Without consistency post-sale, clients may question the sincerity of the trust-building efforts sellers made throughout the sales cycle. For example, when the time that both parties invested in understanding the client's needs and nuances, brainstorming problems and solutions, or predicting how the proposed solution would perform every day in the business is followed by radio silence, it can be jarring. Was all that effort just a means to an end or, rather, to a close? To create more consistent experiences with clients, pre- and post-sale, we can coach salespeople around this habit—which is essentially a fringe gap. We can help them understand the potential client perception and how threading some of the presale attention and insights through post-sale interactions can reduce relationship risks.

THREE BELIEFS

1. You can't spend the same amount of time with everyone, so you have to choose wisely.
2. Strong, timely outreaches don't happen by chance, and you don't have time for unfruitful outreaches.
3. Your formula for alignment is a balance between sincere client interest and self-interest.

While recognizing that watchouts are important, the intervention is essential. Simply recognizing problematic habits only get us so far. Once a salesperson is aware of a gap, they must buy in to the fix. That starts with replacing existing beliefs and ideas. In the absence of an effective belief system, a salesperson will substitute their own notions and ideas—which collectively contributes to inconsistency across a sales team.

Some common examples include the belief that the little things are optional rather than the belief that the little things matter. Or no one is watching, so it's OK to skip over an established step in the sales process, say, conducting a thorough discovery. However, once the right belief system is established, it becomes a beacon that provides the why behind the what. The Diligence Framework brings that standardization to both individual sellers and the sales function as a whole. Each dimension is rooted in three corresponding beliefs and principles that all can rally around.

When it comes to Growing Relationships, the first belief is one of the most important to internalize: *You can't spend the same amount of time with everyone, so you have to choose wisely.* This belief is an antidote to the watchout of prioritizing relationships based on likability, shared social interest, or level of comfort.

It's not to say that there won't be some high-producing client relationships that are also comfortable for the salesperson—these are ideal scenarios. Most often, though, a salesperson needs to run a calculation on what sales activities with whom will get them closer to meeting their revenue goals. To that end, this belief serves as an effective check on how the salesperson needs to think about time allocation.

The second belief is an extension of the first: *Strong, timely outreaches don't happen by chance, and you don't have time for unfruitful outreaches.* Ideal timing plays an important role in sales. This particular belief helps the salesperson focus on their role in bringing about ideal timing with clients. True, there are many things that a salesperson cannot control. They may not be able to expand a client's budget or get a committed dissenter on board. But a salesperson can engage with their clients and get a pulse on the priorities and issues that are brewing in the business. They can follow up that insider information with a series of progressive outreaches over time, which include piquing the client's interest and providing insights. The pattern is simple: the salesperson reaches out with things for the client to consider, quick-gathers any updates or new information, and then waits in the wings until the opportunity ripens.

Salespeople have many accounts and activities that demand their attention, so it's important that they plan and schedule these outreaches in advance but only for the client relationships with the highest potential. Then when the time is right on the client side, the transition from a passive to an active opportunity will feel organic and natural.

While the first two beliefs necessary to Growing Relationships underscore the importance of using time and outreaches wisely, the third belief is in fact an important tactic—it helps salespeople determine which clients to focus on. The key is using alignment as a guide, more specifically: *your formula for alignment is a balance between sincere client interest and self-interest.*

When looking across a territory, a book of accounts, or even a mountain of new leads, salespeople can gain focus and clarity through the continuous habit of seeking alignment. Alignment occurs when the client's interest overlaps with your organization's existing capability and, in some cases, the salesperson's expertise.

For newer relationships, alignment is more about uncovering the potential to work together, whereas for more established relationships, it is about expansion. In either case, the hard work of uncovering or rediscovering client interest and forging that alignment resides with the salesperson as part of their diligent efforts at Growing Relationships.

Chapter 4

Situational Intelligence

Effectively identifies and interprets subtle or overt signals from others during important interactions and makes quick, deliberate adjustments in mindset, approach, or behavior to gain traction and increase personal credibility.

The role of emotional intelligence in driving successful sales outcomes has been popular and validated within published research. For some salespeople, empathy and understanding come naturally. For others, it requires some development. While reading books or attending a training class can teach the theory of emotional intelligence and raise awareness of its importance, the only way for someone to become more skilled in this area is through relentless practice. Emotionally intelligent salespeople have learned to walk a mile in the shoes of their clients. They take on their needs and feelings. Before trying to solve a client's problem, these salespeople put a lot of effort into understanding the problem. People can sense this humanity and appreciate it.

Of course, when practiced at higher levels, emotional intelligence involves understanding how one's behavior impacts another person's style or preferences. When there is a clash or disconnect, it also involves dialing one's behavior up or back depending on what the circumstance calls for.

The second Diligence Dimension, *Situational Intelligence,* includes emotional intelligence, but it goes further in ways that are crucial for sales. While emotional intelligence focuses on the people part of the equation, Situational Intelligence adds another important layer—sales process context. Salespeople who have developed the Situational Intelligence capability not only adapt well to the interpersonal needs of others but also remain keenly aware of clues and cues that tell them whether the sales opportunity they are working is progressing, stalling, or moving backward. In other words, they are attuned to the needs of people and to the integrity of the sales opportunity. When those factors are in sync, people with Situational Intelligence know that good things are just around the corner. However, when there is a disconnect, they adjust their approach to meet the moment and communicate appropriately using their emotional intelligence abilities.

This is a powerful combination and one that is developed gradually. Those salespeople with a strong baseline in emotional intelligence will have an early developmental advantage, though next-level Situational Intelligence insists that these individuals build upon that foundation to thoroughly understand sales process. This knowledge helps a salesperson recognize, in real time, situational indicators that speak to whether a sales opportunity is truly progressing. The final rung of developing Situational Intelligence is to put it all together. Here it is important to confidently navigate the room and drive the right actions based off what the situation requires.

Situational Intelligence covers several fringe gaps that emotional intelligence alone cannot. First, it drives sales process knowledge into the everyday workflow and becomes an easy conversation starter for coaching. As Situational Intelligence becomes a more frequent topic, it starts taking root within the sales function. The concept becomes common language to describe a shared understanding and importance.

Managers need only ask a salesperson about what sort of objective evidence they have to prove that a sales opportunity is at the stage they say it is. So if a salesperson says that a deal is going to close, the manager can probe to understand exactly what the client said and what they committed to that would make the salesperson believe the deal is going to close. Just feeling good about it doesn't work with Situational Intelligence.

This practice of evaluating opportunities based off client evidence strengthens pipeline reporting. When salespeople know they are going to be asked about objective criteria after an interaction, they will start looking for it during their encounters.

THREE WATCHOUTS

1. Having an underdeveloped ability to recognize personal style strengths and challenges
2. Taking a passive approach to reading the room and overlooking important clues that require a style or substance modification
3. Responding to mixed or unfavorable signals by either pushing the original agenda or by dropping back and allowing an unmanaged takeover to occur

One challenge that emerges early is *having an underdeveloped ability to recognize personal style strengths and challenges.* This applies, in particular, to how a salesperson's first and second impressions are perceived by others. This first watchout illustrates what happens when a salesperson has lower levels of emotional intelligence.

Knowing oneself is critically important. It is analogous to getting out of bed in the morning, something everyone has to do if they are going to have a good day.

There are plenty of personality inventory devices or training out there that help salespeople understand their individual styles. In fact, it's more likely than not that you've brought in one of these solutions to help your team. This watchout assumes that a salesperson has some insight into themselves. The focus is on what happens if someone isn't aware of how they come across to others. Being self-aware is a critical component of human interaction, as is recognizing who you're engaging with and adapting behavioral habits to accelerate the speed at which you can forge a connection and pick up traction with another person. The alternative is an interaction that limps along.

This brings to mind what happens with chemical experiments in lab settings. Knowing the characteristics of individual raw material is a good start. However, the scientist guiding the experiment needs a solid understanding of how the raw materials may react as they are mixed. When compounding materials together, the scientist will carefully watch for signs of a positive or negative reaction so that the formula can be either solidified or adjusted accordingly. Salespeople who combine the art of who they are as individuals with the science of fine-tuning their approach to the needs of others are able to open up channels of receptivity that will serve them well throughout the Sales Process.

Another watchout involves *taking a passive approach to reading the room and overlooking important clues that require a style or substance modification.*

Clues either affirm that the salesperson's approach is working or they signal the need to adjust. Picking up on these vital signs starts with the ability to read the room. This action might literally involve scanning a conference room for reactions during a live in-person meeting. Or it could mean doing the same thing but in a virtual setting. These include audio-only phone calls or virtual webcam-type interactions. There are also those times when a salesperson may be meeting face-to-face while one or more stakeholders are videoconferenced in. In these cases, it's too easy to focus more on the person or people in front of you and inadvertently ignore those who have joined remotely. Reading the room, whatever that room may be, starts with observing all participants, their role in the process, what is said, and what isn't said. Salespeople who struggle with this watchout are instead passive about looking for these important clues. As a result, they often miss crucial time-sensitive opportunities to make style or substance adjustments. Instead of capturing the concern and bringing it out into the open, they let that unaddressed matter live on to potentially bloom offline.

While failing to read the room can be a real misstep, the third Situational Intelligence watchout is a real travesty: *responding to mixed or unfavorable signals by either pushing the original agenda or by dropping back and allowing an unmanaged takeover to occur.* Most salespeople recognize when a meeting is going south. Some don't pick up on the signals, but most at least can tell when their original plan for the meeting is disintegrating quickly.

It is common that when things aren't going according to plan, salespeople go into fight-or-flight mode. In front of clients, the attempt to fight looks like digging in on the original plan and attempting to pull others along. Sellers might assume that the client just needs to know more, and so they keep talking. A salesperson might try to introduce new information or feature dump, hoping that something they say will prompt the client to do an about-face. While this Hail Mary technique can work occasionally, it is not situationally intelligent. Instead, this ineffective behavior often feels desperate. It can hurt the salesperson's credibility and weaken their company's position as a viable solution provider.

Speaking of a weakened posture, when salespeople respond to mixed or unfavorable signals by dropping back and allowing the client to run over them, this is a form of flight. They've made a mental retreat. In situations when the client takes the reins and starts dictating, the salesperson has to maintain their position as a partner in the process. Otherwise, too much passivity may turn the salesperson into a completely ineffective order-taker—not a good look nor a position of strength from which to rebuild a sales approach.

THREE BELIEFS

1. Style agility is the one factor over which you have complete control.
2. Cultivating a total intake strategy will help you see real-time adjustments to make.
3. Sometimes you just have to throw out the playbook.

Given how robust the Situational Intelligence dimension is, it is easy to see how it can propel salespeople toward success through the sales process. But it takes some commitment to develop this capability over time. One way to get started fast is by embracing the following three beliefs. The first involves recognizing that *style agility is the one factor over which you have complete control.* At its core, a salesperson's style is how they behave or the energy they give off. Either we're fortunate and our style meshes well with another person, or we need to adjust so that our style works for us, not against us. This adjustment doesn't mean that a salesperson is no longer authentic. What it speaks to is more of a curation or cherry-picking of certain style qualities that will help them click faster with another person. This process is about toning down or dialing up certain qualities based on what someone else needs so that you can create maximum engagement.

When salespeople embrace the fact that they have a strong degree of control when interacting with others, it can change their entire mindset. Rather than believing that their success is predicated on the behavior of others, they can flip that script. Instead of depending on someone else's actions, the salesperson must lean into their ability to influence outcomes by quickly recognizing, adjusting, and connecting with their clients using style agility. This belief can create seller confidence that no matter what situation they encounter, the next move, their reaction, is firmly in their control.

Cultivating a total intake strategy will help you see real-time adjustments to make. This belief is foundational to accepting the need for a heightened awareness throughout client conversations—from open to close. For salespeople who struggle with consistent listening or practicing emotional intelligence, this belief will present a vigorous challenge. In other words, if passive listening lies on one end of the engagement spectrum, committing to a total intake strategy represents its polar opposite. That said, any development change happens gradually, and therefore embracing this belief is a good first step to help salespeople become more sensitive to what is happening around them when they're meeting with clients.

This total intake strategy combines the following factors: where your sales opportunity sits within the overall sales process, your objective for the meeting, overt client reactions, subtle or unspoken reactions, consensus or lack of, and overall tone/energy. A salesperson has developed a total intake strategy when they can observe and analyze these factors in the moment. Doing so will help them understand if they're making the right progress with the client or if things are about to stall out.

Next comes pairing the right sales actions with what the total intake has revealed. If momentum is truly on the salesperson's side, then the next step is to close on the original objective for the meeting. However, if intake indicators point to mixed reactions or brewing concerns, then the salesperson would suspend the original objective and steer the conversation accordingly.

Of course, *sometimes you just have to throw out the playbook.* Situational Intelligence relies on the salesperson being honest with themselves about what is taking place. As things evolve with clients, there will be times when the salesperson has to come to terms with the fact that their original plan won't work in its current form. Maybe the client is signaling that priorities or budgets have shifted. Or perhaps a competitor has surged ahead since the last time the salesperson met with the client. There might even be a new or unexpected stakeholder now involved in the process. Regardless, if newly acquired intelligence is indicating that adjustments need to be made, then it's time to throw out the playbook.

So what then? To avoid the fight-or-flight responses we discussed previously, the best way for a salesperson to respond is to drop back into discovery mode. When new factors emerge in the sales process and the salesperson is situationally attuned, the decision to set aside their original plan demonstrates an openness to understand where the client is. Choosing to meet this uncertainty with some precise questioning can help the conversational tires grip the road again. There's no need to make new promises or solutions during this reset period. Instead, the salesperson can buy themselves time to go back and rethink their approach before reengaging the client.

Chapter 5

Securing Information

Exhibits genuine curiosity to learn and places high value on obtaining, documenting, and leveraging relevant information to uncover context, needs, motivators, and opportunities, with a focused effort to dig for root causes and other critical details that inform next steps.

Client discovery is so crucial for successful selling that any related dimension or competency must be comprehensive enough to define all the related major and minor behaviors associated with it. Simply focusing on things like precall preparation and questioning skills doesn't go far enough to address areas that salespeople really struggle with during client discovery. This is where the Diligence Framework dimension of *Securing Information* comes in. Securing Information covers the common skills and behaviors often associated with client discovery while also covering other lesser-known skills necessary to perform consistently well over time. The dimension name itself speaks to the ways that consultative salespeople must approach their work during discovery.

First, sellers have to secure or procure accurate information from the client. This component of Securing Information tracks closely with prediscovery preparation, personal curiosity (expressed as a personality quality), questioning skills, and techniques. It also includes related soft skills such as gaining feedback. Securing Information has a missional quality about it, a recognition that learning as much as you can about where the client stands is the point of the exercise. This purpose-driven approach naturally guards against tendencies to breeze past this stage and start impatiently pitching solutions to see if something sticks.

Next, Securing Information includes what salespeople need to do with the information they uncovered during client discovery. In this case, the behavior of initially uncovering a wealth of knowledge from the client now extends into an analytic exercise of sorts. The salesperson has to take the time to practice filtering, categorizing, and prioritizing what they've learned. This routine is especially important when the process of client discovery happens over several interactions, including emails, lengthy attachments, or instances where several different people are weighing in with their perspectives. If salespeople don't have the discipline to gather, secure, and make sense of all these inputs, they will put themselves at a disadvantage.

While Securing Information defines the best salesperson behavior for handling client discovery, it disseminates these behaviors in a process-like way. Securing Information speaks to preparing for client discovery, uncovering client information, and both analyzing and safeguarding information. Even before drilling into each of these points for greater clarity, if a salesperson just committed to following that process, in order, each time with their clients, it would infuse consistency into their work.

Of course, looking more deeply into each part of Securing Information reveals a variety of specific ways that salespeople can work through client discovery with excellence. As salespeople meet with clients, they use prepared questions and a methodical approach to learn as much as they can about the client's needs, priorities, and other contributing factors. This live discovery requires focused attention. Salespeople should not be analyzing (filtering, categorizing, and prioritizing) information in real time during the client exchange.

The clearest picture of client needs and how the salesperson's company can solve them will not fully emerge until the salesperson can go back and put all the pieces together. Having as much information as possible increases the probability that a salesperson will offer an accurate response or recommendation to the client during the next meeting. Depending on the specifics of a potential deal, sellers may need to bring other colleagues in to help. When this happens, knowledge transfer is critical. A salesperson must take the time to share the big picture and small client mentions or seemingly unimportant details with their colleagues. This ensures continuity between the client's experience with their salesperson and now with the salesperson's colleagues. In cases where the salesperson shares these details with colleagues who specialize in a particular area, those seemingly unimportant things may actually create a light bulb moment that makes a difference in your company's ability to serve the client.

Also implied within Securing Information is the concept of safeguarding information—something that is as important in life as it is in business. Consider typical human behavior related to valuable things like expensive jewelry. We may tuck it into a fireproof wall safe and in some cases add its appraised value to our homeowner's insurance policy. These actions are common, because items of worth require special attention from their owners. To draw a parallel to sales, what could be more valuable than information about a qualified opportunity that was obtained at the expense of a prospective or current client's time?

The concept of safeguarding information in a way that is thorough and complete is a distinctive measure within the Securing Information dimension.

THREE WATCHOUTS

1. Viewing the collection of (client) information as a means to an end and obtaining the bare minimum required before pitching solutions NO NO
2. Lacking a system for distinguishing between or categorizing information as relevant, indirectly relevant, or not relevant to advancing the opportunity
3. Failing to document relevant information during and immediately after the client interaction as a means to safeguard, share, and use it throughout the sales cycle

While watchouts are often behavioral based, they can also be attitudinal in nature. The first Securing Information watchout is a mix of both behavior and attitude. It involves *viewing the collection of (client) information as a means to an end and obtaining the bare minimum required before pitching solutions.* This can be a common habit and mindset especially with mid- to lower sales performers. Securing Information isn't a warm-up act. Early in the sales process when you need to get traction with the client, Securing Information should be the main act.

A good illustration of how this issue plays out in the real world comes to us from the sales training classroom. Imagine there are three flip charts. One is labeled Strategic Questions, another one Tactical Questions, and a third Other Questions. The salespeople in the room are given a marker and asked to write down one to two of their best real-life questions in each category. To avoid repetition, the participants are asked to star or upvote instances where someone else already wrote down the question they were going to contribute. By the time everyone goes around the room, you should, in theory, have a master collection of group questions across each of the three flip charts. But in reality, one or two scenarios are more likely to play out. On the one hand, you may see that all three flip charts, regardless of their labeling, largely contain tactical questions. Two-thirds of those questions will be close ended, which are problematic because that structure will shut down the client discussion, not keep it open.

On the other hand, some training groups might include three to four good questions on the Strategic flip chart; however, by contrast, the Tactical and Other Questions pages will be so full that people start writing sideways with itty-bitty letters just to jam in one more tactical question. When salespeople are asked to role-play these questions, the results are also predictable. The tactical questions are so to the point that when they are asked in succession, the approach feels choppy, not conversational.

Yet when a salesperson role-plays asking some strategic questions, you can feel the nervous energy in the room. The salesperson is outside their comfort zone, big time. They are essentially putting themselves out there, and the client might respond with something that the seller cannot address in the moment. However, the wealth of information that comes from asking a strategic question is far more revealing than simply asking a string of tactical questions. Overcoming this watchout requires, in most cases, simply a genuine belief that client information is extraordinarily valuable and that sales success in large part is connected to the volume and quality of these insights.

Speaking of quality, while salespeople should focus on information capture during client discovery, not all of it warrants immediate action after the fact. Without the means to determine what information is actionable and what is merely reference, the salesperson might miss something important. Therefore, the next major watchout is *lacking a system for distinguishing between or categorizing information as relevant, indirectly relevant, or not relevant to advancing the opportunity.*

The sheer volume of information uncovered during client discovery can be overwhelming without a system. When you take into account all the details that can add up among internet research, potential prior CRM notes, true open-ended questioning, and anything additional a client might send over or share, that's a lot to track and organize. Without a method for quickly sifting through and making sense of this information, salespeople tend to revert back to the most memorable or recent details a client provided. The most recent details are easier to recall, but that doesn't mean they are the most relevant.

Averting this watchout requires the realization that what a salesperson does with client information is just as important as gathering the information in the first place. Categorizing information goes hand in hand with documenting and safeguarding it.

The final obstacle to Securing Information is also related to challenges in working with client information. This watchout is in play when *failing to document relevant information during and immediately after the client interaction as a means to safeguard, share, and use it throughout the sales cycle.*

One good practice would be keeping a worksheet with the current sales objective at the top. Underneath that header would be three columns, or it could be three corresponding pages if you need more space. Label your far-left column or first page Directly Relevant, meaning any information that follows directly connects with advancing the current sales objective. Label the middle column or second page Indirectly Relevant. Here you'll list any client information that isn't immediately actionable but may be useful in the future. It could also include details about indirect stakeholders or other business issues. These notes may not need to be directly addressed in a current solution or proposal, but you should review them frequently throughout the sales cycle. Label the far-right column or third page Not Relevant. This should include information that is extraneous or unconnected, but since you gathered the information during client discovery, it would be a best practice to categorize and retain. Without these efforts to secure, safeguard, and share information, a salesperson is essentially fumbling in the dark as they try to move their client opportunities forward.

THREE BELIEFS

1. Genuine curiosity builds trust and gives you an information advantage.
2. Client concerns or confusion that aren't unearthed today become tomorrow's concrete objections.
3. Safeguarding and presiding over information inventory is a personal differentiator.

Given the importance of Securing Information and the different facets that make up this dimension, developing this capability takes commitment and practice. For many salespeople, the first step involves thinking through their belief system. Before they will be motivated to do the work required, they have to believe that *genuine curiosity builds trust and gives you an information advantage.*

It takes a lot of effort and energy to prepare and then lead open, potentially uncontrollable conversations about what's important to the client. Then it takes real discipline to sift through that detail and categorize it well. When salespeople choose to go further than those at competitive companies, prospective clients often notice. They utter that phrase we recognize as going above and beyond. Creating this reputation starts with curiosity.

Salespeople can get the ball rolling on outworking their competition by showing the client how much they care about their needs, priorities, and other contributing factors. They can double down on that trust building by inviting the client to be candid, even if what's shared is hard to hear. It takes a certain measure of boldness to request that a client share their unfiltered thoughts—these are the practices that make up next-level selling.

Salespeople will rise to this occasion when they recognize that a moment of being uncomfortable can lead to greater gains down the line. This mindset demonstrates the second important belief related to Securing Information, which is that *client concerns or confusion that aren't unearthed today become tomorrow's concrete objections.* When sticking points arise early on in the Sales Process, they are much easier to tackle. In most cases, both parties are just starting to invest in the potential working relationship. The client hasn't gone on the record yet in support of a solution and the associated time or dollar commitment, so the stakes are lower—there's often less angst or tension when challenging issues surface.

It's sort of like two single people jumping into the dating scene. One reason is to find a great life partner. Maybe the goal is to eventually get married and have children. When two seemingly compatible people meet, their first few dates are probably lighthearted and easygoing. Chances are serious topics like family planning won't come up early on, but if they do, any initial disagreements are much easier to talk through than they are after the couple has invested a few years of their life in the relationship. If a friend of yours was in this situation, you would probably advise them to broach these important subjects before buying an expensive ring or moving in.

So too should salespeople recognize that client concerns and issues are best uncovered early and often. They need to do the work to dig around the client's philosophy, expectations, potential supporters or critics, viewpoints on time, budget, terms, internal or infrastructure hurdles, and competitive comparisons, including the choice to insource.

Once the salesperson has uncovered candid client information along with other critical details, it is important that they believe that *safeguarding and presiding over information inventory is a personal differentiator.* If knowing a client's needs, priorities, and contributing factors is important to recommending the right solution, then securing that information is a must. When salespeople believe that safekeeping information can set their personal selling brand apart, they will build time into their schedule to transfer details out of their memory, phone, pad, or notebook. They will systematically build the client record after every interaction into a thorough and orderly reflection of both current and future opportunities for your company. Doing so also makes retrieving information easy and predictable for themselves and others. When practiced collectively by the sales organization, this discipline alone will be a game changer.

Chapter 6

Intentional Listening

Expresses a sincere interest in others and remains in a receiving mode to effectively capture, interpret, and confirm the meaning and intent behind spoken words, emotional tone, and other critical nonverbal cues.

Listening and related behaviors are a staple in nearly all competency models, and sales research routinely cites them as essential skills. It would seem like everything that can be said about listening is already out there. Really, who doesn't know that listening is important? When most people think about this skill within a sales context, what comes to mind are its different types: passive versus active or hearing versus listening. While slight nuances differentiate each type, most people would describe *passive* or *hearing* as a lower-engagement, selective type of listening.

By contrast, *active* or *listening* (as the opposite of hearing) are often associated with sellers who are more engaged in the listening process. These salespeople may be more observational, taking note of the nonverbal cues that a client gives off. They might also put their listening into action by paraphrasing or feeding back to the client what they heard them say. This type of level-one listening is indeed a very important part of fundamental selling skills.

As salespeople move beyond the fundamentals and become more skilled, they will likely adopt a consistent preparation routine. This discipline is important, because having a plan for each client interaction keeps the sales process moving along. When working their plan with clients, these higher-performing salespeople are also more likely to up their listening game. As they ask the questions they've prepared, these salespeople are locked into each aspect of their client's response to uncover key information. I call this listening with intent, or Intentional Listening.

As a Diligence Dimension, Intentional Listening is more purpose driven than its active listening predecessor. This heightened state of listening happens when the salesperson's behavior evolves from practicing a skill to making listening a part of their proactive sales strategy. This means that a salesperson will expand their preparation routine. Ahead of an important meeting, the salesperson will take the time to determine two things: the questions they will ask *and* the specific things they will listen for. When salespeople become intentional about listening, they assign the same level of importance to their listening approach as they do to their strategic questioning efforts. It evolves from more of an in-the-moment, semiconscious reaction into a fully conscious, proactive practice.

When salespeople implement Intentional Listening well, they consider where they are in the sales process and what client evidence they need to obtain to ensure that their deal is advancing to the next stage. Then they will go into their client interactions looking for clear signals, such as confirmation, validation, or even concerns, to get a strong gauge on where things are.

Intentional Listening takes discipline and practice. While the salesperson most certainly has an agenda going into a client interaction, if they are going to remain in receiving mode, they have to strike a balance of pursuing their agenda rather than pushing it. For example, they may assert an agenda point but then proactively drop back to take in the complete client response. They will look for any disconnects between the words being spoken and nonverbals. As a salesperson absorbs and combines both elements together in real time, they can respond to the client in the most accurate way possible.

In this and other related ways, Intentional Listening is a critical conduit to Situational Intelligence. These two dimensions share a great dependency on one another, as this well-developed listening capability is vital to the quality of the salesperson's total intake strategy, which activates Situational Intelligence.

THREE WATCHOUTS

1. Verbally dominating the conversation, breaking through any momentary pauses or silence by either repeating previous information or introducing something new
2. Lacking interest or willingness to explore conversational undertones or subtext, perhaps fearing a setback
3. Selectively listening for the purposes of validating a preferred agenda and therefore dismiss statements or signals that run contrary to that agenda

Despite its power and potential, there are often low levels of awareness around Intentional Listening behaviors. Add to that some real obstacles and watchouts, and it can be difficult for salespeople to move past the status quo of their natural tendencies. Identifying common watchouts continues to be an important first step in helping salespeople realize how essential it is to maximize all opportunities to listen. The first one is particularly observable. It identifies a pesky habit that effectively shuts down the client information valve. This watchout is nearly always in play because salespeople are often *verbally dominating the conversation, breaking through any momentary pauses or silence by either repeating previous information or introducing something new.*

Have you ever had an interview for a new role during which the person who is supposed to be assessing your candidacy instead talks about themselves the entire time? If you've experienced this before, you know how puzzling it is. Especially after the fact if you hear back from your main contact that the interviewer really liked you and felt you should advance in the process. Total head-scratcher. On what set of facts did this person base their opinion, when you couldn't get a word in edgewise during the interview? Of course, you likely made the best of the situation. Perhaps you looked for opportunities to jump in and demonstrate your preparation and fitness for the role. Though if you were being honest, it didn't seem like there was enough airtime to accurately cover the value you would bring.

Clients react similarly when salespeople have a listening deficit. While many are polite and will allow this behavior to continue to a point, soon one of two things will happen. First, the client may permanently retreat from the conversation, offering no more information and looking for a way to wind it down quickly. Or, if the salesperson keeps dominating the conversation, the client might match the moment with similar (perceived) aggression and push back to ensure that their needs, now likely expressed as demands, are heard. Either scenario threatens the potential for success. The origins of this watchout are frequently psychological. It often comes down to two root causes—low confidence or the deep need for control.

When salespeople have low confidence about their knowledge or abilities, they may inadvertently filibuster the client and repetitively stick with the talking points they're most comfortable with. That means there isn't a lot of room for the client to take the conversation outside of the salesperson's safety zone. When the interaction eventually does begin traveling outside the lines, the salesperson may go on defense. They will pull the conversation backward by retreading prior ground, essentially creating a cul-de-sac dialogue that does little to advance the opportunity.

Similarly, salespeople who need to feel in control will also try to steer the client discussion. Obtaining and maintaining control directly contributes to the second Intentional Listening watchout, which is *lacking interest or willingness to explore conversational undertones or subtext, perhaps fearing a setback.*

When a salesperson with controlling tendencies sees a pause in the action with a client, instead of letting it hang out there for a moment, they will interrupt the silence. They perceive silence as a potential risk to their agenda. The salesperson might worry that during the pause, the client begins thinking about reasons that the salesperson's proposal won't work or begins fixating on something else that might cause a setback. Of course, the inclination to interrupt might also be a die-hard, used-car-style sales habit that has gone unchecked for too long. Regardless, whether the root cause of dominating the sales conversation is one of confidence or control, this watchout does not create the necessary space for Intentional Listening. It also most likely ends up annoying the client.

The final watchout occurs when salespeople are *selectively listening for the purposes of validating a preferred agenda and therefore dismiss statements or signals that run contrary to that agenda.* This half-hearted attempt at listening is essentially confirmation bias in action. The salesperson puts a disproportionate amount of weight on the client's words and actions that validate their preferred outcome. They downplay or dismiss indications that run contrary to what they want to see happen. Unfortunately, this type of selective listening only serves to distort reality for the salesperson. By ignoring undesirable signals, the seller does not confront potential issues that can come roaring back down the line.

When salespeople push their original plans on clients instead of developing an approach in which they stay flexible to what they learn, it compromises their chance for success. Even if a deal were to close in spite of driving an agenda, how strong will the longer-term client relationship be without a consistent listening practice?

THREE BELIEFS

1. Listening is a choice to be made over and over again.
2. All conversations require a climb up the listening ladder.
3. Silence really is golden, so it's important to pay close attention to what you hear next.

Intentional Listening together with the other dimensions of Securing Information and Situational Intelligence form a perfect triangle of knowledge and empowerment. These combined behaviors help a salesperson recognize where they are in the sales process, what the client needs, and what actions they should take next. Of course, when salespeople start getting more serious about their listening skills, they will quickly discover that there are no shortcuts. Next-level listening simply requires time and practice. Embracing a set of related beliefs will create the right mindset and support the desire to excel in this area.

The first belief is rather straightforward but equally significant: *Listening is a choice to be made over and over again.* The fact is that Intentional Listening doesn't always come naturally for salespeople, especially competitive ones. There can be this misnomer that if you are dominating, then you are winning. However, the choice to sideline your agenda for a moment to truly hear what another person is saying is, in and of itself, pretty powerful. A choice to listen is also an inclusive one. When a salesperson decides to listen, they are sending a clear message that the client's thoughts, viewpoints, or concerns are just as important as their own plan. That give / take / internalize dynamic will advance a sales opportunity much faster than when a salesperson tries to barrel down a one-way track.

With this in mind, another important belief takes into account that *all conversations require a climb up the listening ladder.* In other words, it is a rather gradual journey. Listening can and should be more science than art, and one way to apply this belief is to visualize listening as a ladder. There are essentially three rungs: hearing, understanding, and translating.

Hearing is merely a starting point. It focuses only on what the client is verbally saying. The next step up on the ladder brings us to understanding. This involves taking in all client signals (words, tone, nonverbals). Together hearing and understanding form the basis of what most people would consider to be solid, fundamental listening skills.

However, there is one more rung on the ladder. The final step involves the salesperson translating what they heard and understood from the client into action—this represents the very core of Intentional Listening. Translating is the more advanced skill of analysis and feedback. Here the salesperson demonstrates their ability to pick up on common client reactions (confirmation, confusion, or concern) and guide the conversation accordingly.

Silence really is golden, so it's important to pay close attention to what you hear next. This final belief also serves as a note of caution for salespeople—most specifically the talkative ones. Curbing the natural tendency to dominate a sales conversation and snuff out moments of silence is hard for a lot of people. Fully realizing the power of silence can help.

Certain personal styles need silence to create space in the conversation. When clients allow silence to set in during an interaction, they may be preparing a response or taking a moment to indulge their inner dialogue. If that's the case, ending the silence prematurely can be detrimental to forward progress. When a client has paused and the discussion has become momentarily quiet, the best action a salesperson can take is to drop back and stay in receiving mode.

Silence can also create some positive, atmospheric tension. This is especially true during negotiation when, as the old adage says, he who speaks first loses. When you let silence run its course, whatever comes next from the client will have greater importance, more so than anything you might manage to ferret out prematurely. With discipline and practice, a salesperson can learn how to manage silence and use it to their advantage. It starts with the belief that doing so is important.

Chapter 7

Persuasive Communication

Formulates an idea, position, plan, or solution by combining business context with learned insights and articulates the message with clarity, substance, and personal conviction to influence and gain the commitment of others.

When people typically think of selling, what often comes to mind is the ability to influence and persuade. At its core, being able to convince another person that your recommendation or solution is the best fit for their needs is where the rubber meets the road.

The Diligence Dimension of Persuasive Communication is comprehensive. It knits together the traditional elements of persuasion, presentation, and influence into one finely tuned competency. As a sales leader who's observed many seller interactions throughout your career, chances are good that you can immediately recognize salespeople who excel in this area. These individuals effortlessly persuade others to take the actions they want. While this mastery of skill comes naturally to some, by defining all the behaviors that factor into Persuasive Communication, we can help salespeople who are strong persuaders maximize this ability and support improvement in others who may be less skilled.

It's important to communicate persuasively throughout the sales cycle, and the more an opportunity develops and is ready for prime time, the more critical this skill set becomes.

While Persuasive Communication is important throughout the sales cycle, when the time comes to pitch a solution, this ability is mission-critical. The salesperson's messaging has to be tight, crisp, and on point—sort of like opening night at the theater. After months of rigorous practice and buildup, a lead actor is ready to take the stage for a long-anticipated, sold-out performance. The skills of their craft must be on full display to move the audience. It's a now-or-never sort of performance dynamic brought about by the right timing and the need to deliver well.

After the salesperson has validated a sales opportunity, that is to say there is a need, the time comes to present a solution for consideration. Following a successful presentation, these same persuasion efforts should continue on through to the official close. Ahead of presenting, the salesperson should follow a disciplined preparation routine. They must do the legwork of taking the components of their company's offering and building messaging points around it. It is important to factor in how the client is most likely to consume the message. As a tastier visual, let's correlate this idea to building an ice-cream sundae. We'll look at how an ideal message comes together, using both a business and a dessert example to observe the parallel in the approach.

First, let's break down the messaging components a seller would typically have to work with and, for fun, correlate them to some sweet ingredients. This starts with the core solution your company has to offer. This is essentially what you have to propose that will meet a client's needs. Likewise, we'll say that the base of the yet-to-be-personalized ice-cream sundae is just three scoops of vanilla ice cream in the bottom of a glass dish. If the seller presented just your core solution to a client (unmodified in any way) or if a patron was given just three scoops of vanilla ice cream in a bowl, neither makes for a particularly palatable or persuasive offering. Fortunately, there are more client insights and sundae ingredients to work with.

As the salesperson continues preparing their message around the core solution, we'll assume that through questioning, the client revealed how important it is for them to buy into a good service package (hot fudge) in addition to any core solution.

Perhaps the client also shared that quantifying a good value or internal costs savings (nuts on top of the ice cream) was another factor weighing on their buying decision. Finally, let's say that the client also mentioned that having access to resources they could use to speed up team knowledge internally would be ideal but not required (cherries). Using both the sundae illustration and the sales scenario, Persuasive Communication-type messaging might look like this:

Personalized Sundae	Tailored Solution
I know you have been looking forward to dessert, so I took our three homemade scoops of vanilla ice cream and sat them atop a layer of our warm hot fudge and drizzled some on top as well—you can never have enough of that goodness. I also included our crushed salted peanuts and, last but not least, a tangy cherry on top. Our best-selling dessert, built just the way you like it.	I want to share with you how our core solution combined with our gold-level support package can meet your needs today and grow with you over the next two to three years. By implementing this solution, we estimate that you will save 25 percent in time and money over insourcing, which I know is important to you. Finally, I'm going to show you our vast on-demand knowledge base to educate your internal team. This package curates the best we have to offer in a way that is most relevant to the goals you have shared with me.

At the heart of the Persuasive Communication capability is the willingness and discipline to execute on a repeatable formula. This ability in action is far more about consistency and discipline than it is about advanced skills. Whether they are preparing to pitch or delivering their messaging to a client, a salesperson is at the top of their persuasion game when they can combine the highlights of what they've learned from the client with the most relevant points of their solution and deliver them in order. It is as simple as "I heard you say that ____ matters. Our solution offers 1___, 2___, and 3___ to address that priority." The most influential sellers prepare a side-by-side listing of these points and deliver them with conviction, soliciting the client's feedback and reactions along the way.

Obtaining client confirmation or ferreting out concerns is important for gradually building momentum and enthusiasm for the salesperson's recommendations. When salespeople embrace tough client questions or pushback that comes on the heels of a solution presentation, they increase their credibility and influence. Even if doing so requires a retreat and regroup before engaging with the client again. Despite what might seem like a momentary setback, a salesperson's willingness to deliver a tailored message, invite unfiltered reactions, and advance the opportunity is a disciplined and methodical approach that positions the salesperson as a formidable opponent to any competitor.

The same process of Persuasive Communication, which primarily starts with solution presentation, is also threaded throughout the closing process. Here the salesperson uses the same formula to combine the highlights of what has transpired across the sales process up to that point. They describe the journey that both seller and client have partnered on and set up the final agreement as the next logical action step. When they execute Persuasive Communication well, the salesperson is able to ride the wave of momentum that began during the solution presentation all the way through to a successful close.

THREE WATCHOUTS

1. Relying too strongly on personal style and charisma, without using learned insights or information to add the necessary substance to a message or presentation
2. Failing to order and sequence a message according to what is most important to the client
3. Sticking to the script and digging in or potentially growing defensive when faced with pushback or objections that threaten to derail progress

Given that many salespeople are inherently wired to persuade others, it's easy to lean on one's natural ability in this area. In fact, some people are so confident that they develop a habit of winging it with clients. Both of these realities contribute to common Persuasive Communication watchouts. More specifically, salespeople may be *relying too strongly on personal style and charisma, without using learned insights or information to add the necessary substance to a message or presentation.* If you unravel the origins of this watchout, you discover that somewhere along the way, the salesperson has come to believe that most people do business with them because they are likable. They might say things such as "My clients are loyal; they love me." While that might be true to some degree, as the marketplace has grown more complex and more data driven with greater team consensus around decision-making, strictly doing business on personal preferences alone isn't practical anymore. Sellers who are naturally endowed with charisma must add consistency and discipline around their messaging so that they can win and maintain their client relationships.

Another watchout speaks more to how a salesperson uses messaging to persuade clients. They run into challenges when *failing to order and sequence a message according to what is most important to the client.* Here is another quick sales training illustration on just how chronic this watchout is. There is a training team who, for two years' worth of sales workshops, would ask salespeople to identify themselves as either beach or nature lovers when it came to their ideal vacation. Soon Team Beach and Team Nature would congregate around flip charts as they listed what they thought were the best aspects of their favorite vacation, be it leisure or adventure.

Next, each team was to do a five-minute pitch for a panel of three neutral judges on why their favorite vacation was the better choice. In this contest, the most persuasive group wins. As each group was itemizing their features and benefits sets, the judges would walk around the room and share two or three things they were hoping for in a vacation. When it came time to observe the pitches, the judges were waiting to see if any or all of their shared wishes would show up in either team's messaging. What Team Beach and Team Nature didn't know was that greater weighting would be given to the group that factored in feedback from the judges during their presentations.

What followed next was shockingly predictable. Class after class, each group sent to the front of the room their most fun representative or their most serious and responsible team captain to take the lead on the pitch. Time after time, each team's pitch was essentially a feature dump of the activities that *they* loved the most. While occasionally someone who got the point of the exercise included the judge's preferences in their messaging, this was the exception and not the rule. The vast majority of presentations, while enjoyable, were not relevant to the stated needs and wants. The participants flat-out missed the mark.

While tailored messaging requires discipline to create and

deliver, salespeople still need to be open and flexible during the client interaction. Instead, when salespeople hold on for dear life to their prepared messaging, it shuts the client down. When sellers are simply *sticking to the script and digging in or potentially growing defensive when faced with pushback or objections that threaten to derail progress*, they have a watchout that needs attention. One of the ways to guard against this behavior is to double down on preparation efforts. As salespeople think through and develop their messaging, they can review what they've learned so far about the client and anticipate any number of questions or concerns that may arise. Taking the time to think through these scenarios in advance can help the salesperson steady themselves in the client meeting and go in with the confidence to respond proactively and positively to all manner of feedback.

THREE BELIEFS

1. There's a defined line between being pushy and being persuasive.
2. Always arrange the message in the order that matters most to the client.
3. It serves a seller's interest to invite and engage challenging questions and concerns.

When salespeople combine their natural persuasive abilities with some Persuasive Communication best practices, they can more quickly educate and influence clients to take action. It starts with understanding that *there's a defined line between being pushy and being persuasive.* Without realizing it, salespeople cross that line to their own detriment. Staying on the persuasive side requires some ground rules around message development and delivery—at its core, Persuasive Communication boils down to well-informed and well-timed messaging.

When a salesperson has been working on a sales opportunity and it has picked up some momentum, it's important to invest time in working on both the substance and the style of their messaging. This is the single most important tool they have to win clients over. Developing message substance starts by packaging up what the salesperson has learned about the client. This includes needs, priorities, and other contributing factors. Next, the salesperson should combine those points with the relevant aspects of their solution.

Once they've clarified the substance of this message, it's time to deliver. Salespeople can deliver their messaging effectively by leaning into their style strengths and staying on point. They need to present their focused and precise message with confidence.

It's also important for salespeople to take their cue from the client. After hearing a sales pitch, the client will react either positively, neutrally, or negatively to what was said. To prepare in advance for any one of these reactions, the salesperson should decide that, regardless of how the client behaves, they will choose to lean in and take the time to explore the client's viewpoint. This small but powerful habit ensures that the salesperson will stay in the persuasion zone and not inadvertently wander into pushy territory.

Given how central strong messaging is to consistent, Persuasive Communication, another guiding principle must be this: *Always arrange the message in the order that matters most to the client.* This belief is a silver bullet of sorts. It effectively eliminates most of the bad habits associated with Persuasive Communication watchouts. Salespeople must recognize how important it is to manage the client's interest and their time. With so much competition for a client's attention, their interest and time are often in short supply. Salespeople have to observe and treat these things as the valuable resources they are when delivering a presentation. Capturing the client's attention early and keeping it can be as simple as a salesperson articulating what they heard the client has said (during prior interactions) and linking that information to how their company's approach or solution fits. This belief cuts straight to the heart of the matter because it points to the important role that salespeople play in connecting the dots for clients.

The final belief continues digging in to maximizing persuasiveness, especially during client reaction time. It is important for salespeople to embrace the idea that *it serves a seller's interest to invite and engage challenging questions and concerns* throughout the client dialogue. The adrenaline that comes from a good pitch offers many salespeople a great high. However, if these feelings of euphoria aren't managed, they can cause a salesperson to lose focus and ignore client signals. The most common example happens when a client objects to something a salesperson has said.

In these moments the salesperson has to manage their emotions and agenda. They need to calmly and elegantly pivot away from the prepared talking points and open-mindedly engage the client. The salesperson's influence and persuasion abilities will grow as they work through the client's candid feedback. This honest discussion helps the salesperson draw out how the client really feels about the solution. While this may be momentarily uncomfortable, it is a much better alternative than dealing in half-truths, which makes it very difficult to maintain momentum and traction. When salespeople gain honest insights from a client, it affords them the opportunity to go back and make strategic adjustments to their recommendation.

Chapter 8

Personal Ownership

Espouses responsibility and accountability for any outcome that lies within one's personal span of control, with emphasis on timely, quality work and keeping commitments.

Ask anyone who has had to manage a team, and chances are they would agree that one of the most challenging types of people to manage are those who lack accountability. Unaccountable salespeople are no exception.

Diagnosing the root of accountability or lack thereof is more a matter of character over skill set. The Diligence Framework tackles this developmental area through the dimension of Personal Ownership. It is the first in a series of personal leadership dimensions that supports consistent behavior and elevates sales performance. Before a salesperson can lead clients or colleagues or eventually others in a management role, they have to master leading themselves first. Personal Ownership is a cornerstone of personal leadership.

Given the tight connection between accountability and a person's character, developing Personal Ownership might be a sensitive area for some. However, it is too important to ignore. Low levels of accountability lead to several fringe gaps across the organization. The two most obvious ones are sidestepping sales process expectations and careless handoffs to internal colleagues. Both of these may be subtle, but they are always subversive.

For a salesperson to behave accountably, it is critical that they internalize the idea that whatever falls within their span of control is their responsibility. Accountable people don't utter the words, "That's not my job." Whether that ownership is as small as exerting influence or as significant as single-handedly guiding a matter or issue to its best conclusion, accountable salespeople don't take a selective approach to their work. One easy way to spot accountable people is to look for those who won't defend or deflect their mistakes onto others.

Of course, there are some broader cultural trends that play a role in how accountable some people are. Our modern world has become highly focused on the individual—one's own needs, wants, preferences, triggers, and realities. In moderation, there is nothing wrong with being mindful of those unique qualities that make us who we are. What we have to watch for is when individual focus increases to a point of saturation.

We often hear the phrase "speaking my truth." Of course, the very definition of truth exists to screen out individual subjectivity, so really the concept behind that common assertion is more about relativism. In other words, an individual's own take on a set of facts versus the facts themselves. Recognizing this undercurrent is important because it can subtly permeate our sales teams as well. When this potent individualism reaches critical mass, it naturally harms our efforts at driving consistency across the team. If we allow too much self-focus and personal interpretation of clear directives, then it becomes more difficult to identify areas of lower accountability.

Personal Ownership defines the individual behavior that supports the collective good. A fundamental way to build a bridge from self-interest to being accountable is to make and keep commitments—to clients, to colleagues, your manager, and the business at large. When salespeople own their work and outcomes, they will go on record as the responsible party. They will proactively seek and solve issues all the while distinguishing themselves professionally through more consistent sales performance, stronger client relationships, and overall exceptional character.

THREE WATCHOUTS

1. Assigning greater importance to client-facing spotlight moments than behind-the-scenes tasks that seem less critical
2. Operating apart from established internal standards (pre-/post-sales process), especially when those expectations interfere with personal style and preferences
3. Owning their wins but quickly distancing themselves from their failures

Breaking through individualistic tendencies and becoming more accountable can be challenging, but one way to do so effectively is to identify watchouts. While the examples that follow are most relevant within a sales context, the essence of each can certainly apply to those in non-sales roles as well.

The first watchout operates subtly but with time can take root and impact not only the individual seller but also the sales team at large. It is most common when a salesperson is *assigning greater importance to client-facing spotlight moments than behind-the-scenes tasks that seem less critical.* In other words, the salesperson believes that they are paid just to show up well in front of clients. Therefore, any other responsibility or activity that comes before or after the client interaction is far less important and should fall to someone else. When a salesperson behaves this way, they send a message to others about what work is important and what is menial. Even if your sales team has support people to help level load the work and run point on nonclient-facing activities, a salesperson should still maintain interest and some involvement. This could look like a bit of coaching or encouragement for their colleagues. The reality is that it's a serious watchout when salespeople start calling the shots around what is worthy of their attention and what isn't. This behavior not only becomes ingrained but also stresses out others, and things fall through the cracks.

Another Personal Ownership watchout is in effect when we see a salesperson *operating apart from established internal standards (pre-/post-sales process), especially when those expectations interfere with personal style and preferences.* This pattern shows up in what we would describe as rogue salespeople, and it stems from the same attitudinal issues as the first watchout. People who are preoccupied with their own preferences not only will seek the spotlight moments for themselves but also will shun any internal expectations that cramp their style. When one or two salespeople behave in this way, it is a nuisance to their manager. But when those individuals export this behavior to the rest of the sales team, it creates a serious systemic issue. This behavioral pattern is the polar opposite of Personal Ownership. When salespeople operate outside of established expectations and for all intents and purposes do their own thing, what they are displaying is personal disownership.

To illustrate this concept, imagine that a newer salesperson, who had put a few wins on the board at a professional services firm, has continued pursuing her personal preferences. Despite being told by management to direct her efforts elsewhere, this salesperson continues to pursue third-party channel sales. She whips up these opportunities and puts pressure on management to make an exception to the strategy, asserting that these channel sales would bring in short-term revenue and eventually lead to core sales. When one department manager says no, she goes to another one, politicking her way through the organization to try to get her yes. At one point, three different department managers share notes with one another and conclude that they had each spent more than twenty hours over the last three to four weeks with this individual, trying to both reel her in and work through these unwanted channel deals in progress. Finally, one of the managers expresses that even if these deals were to close, the company systems are not built to provide third-party access—a detail that isn't widely known internally. In the end, all this has been a giant waste of internal time. It is but one example of how individualism can compromise an entire operation.

The final watchout involves adopting self-preservation measures. In this case a salesperson is *owning their wins but quickly distancing themselves from their failures.* This watchout points to a salesperson's selectivity around what they are willing to take credit for rather than owning all outcomes. Just like welcoming spotlight client moments but escaping routine drudgery, owning wins without accepting responsibility for losses is at best dysfunctional and at worst toxic. If a salesperson is quick to credit themselves only with wins, then what are the chances that they are genuinely sharing that glory with other internal colleagues? Likewise, if they divorce themselves from failures, at whose feet do they lie? These self-preservation measures become tiresome over time and can drain the morale of others—not to mention the fact that when salespeople with this watchout don't allow themselves to shoulder a loss, they actually deprive themselves of opportunities to reflect, learn, and grow.

THREE BELIEFS

1. Trade a pass-the-buck mentality for a the-buck-stops-with-me mindset.
2. Mastering process puts your ownership efforts into overdrive.
3. Own the failures as much as the wins.

Exploring your sales team's belief system around Personal Ownership can collectively help address what otherwise may be a challenging topic. There is psychological safety in groups, which allows an individual some space to consider how modifying their belief system could serve them well professionally. Owning work outcomes for better or worse has a major upside—it is the epitome of personal power. No longer is someone a victim of circumstances. Instead, there's a bold recognition that a salesperson controls what happens to them and can choose to extract lessons when outcomes are less than ideal.

With this in mind, the first Personal Ownership belief means that you *trade a pass-the-buck mentality for a the-buck-stops-with-me mindset.* When confronted with broader issues that seem outside of a salesperson's immediate responsibilities, the choice is clear. Operating with Personal Ownership will cause a salesperson to own the full gamut of activities surrounding client interactions, not just the spotlight moments. For things that do get passed off on colleagues, the salesperson can still own their role to capture, communicate, and shepherd outcomes or coach and encourage others on the team. The choice to adopt this mindset not only makes good collegial working relationships but also positively impacts clients. When a client realizes that a salesperson owns their issues, even if other team members attend to the details, their credibility increases, and over time the client comes to see them as a trusted adviser.

Mastering process puts your ownership efforts into overdrive. It is tempting to view sales and internal process as optional. However, process simply defines what it looks like when things get done right. When process is circumvented, activities may still happen, but the way these things unfold may be incomplete, confusing, or frustrating for all involved. On the flip side, when a salesperson adopts this belief, they are essentially changing the way they view process. While this change in mindset and practice might be challenging at first, over time salespeople will see how following process helps them operate with greater intelligence and produce far better outcomes.

The final belief is a simple call to action. *Own the failures as much as the wins.* Sometimes promising opportunities fizzle away. Or sometimes things go wrong with clients. When actual experiences fall short of expectation, the salesperson has an opportunity to build trust in the trenches. Most clients aren't looking for perfection; they are looking for ownership. How well a salesperson navigates failures and setbacks says far more to most clients about their professionalism than when things go according to plan.

While the origins of Personal Ownership are character based, our belief system is the gateway to developing new patterns of behavior. When salespeople begin owning all the outcomes within their span of control, it will collectively strengthen the sales team as a whole. You will start seeing salespeople personally facilitating strong handoffs internally for important matters, even if those issues are outside of their job description. They will do this because they care about the outcome more than about drawing lines around what is or is not their job.

As these individuals become more invested in strong, consistent outcomes, you will see them staying on top of any unresolved issues until they come to a satisfactory close. As a direct result of cultivating individual and collective Personal Ownership within your sales teams, instead of dealing with nuisance habits or behaviors, there will be a recognition of how sellers maintain a high level of reliability and can be counted on to follow through on expectations and commitments. As the first leadership dimension on the journey toward seller excellence, everything else hinges off Personal Ownership.

Chapter 9

Time Planning

Maintains a broad view of personal workload at all times and utilizes a prioritization method to balance both proactive and reactive activities according to the highest and best use of time necessary to achieve expected levels of performance.

Time is a salesperson's most valuable and limited resource. As a second personal leadership dimension, Time Planning serves as a more comprehensive competency than its close cousin, Time Management. When developing newer or under-performing salespeople, it is critical that they learn to manage their time well. However, when a seller reaches a more intermediate or advanced level, the process of being more proactive at approaching the use of time becomes part of their personal sales strategy, and, of course, the higher performing a salesperson is, the more valuable they are to their organization. There are just certain high performers who managers wish they could clone. Since it's hard to do that, the best way to extract more revenue from these successful salespeople is to further improve the way that they deploy their time. The behaviors and actions associated with Time Planning provide a road map for this.

Drilling into the nuances between time management and

Time Planning a bit more, time management involves more of a defensive strategy to ensure that a salesperson can get to their list of pressing issues and important activities. It's highly tactical in nature. Time Planning combines the tactics of time management with a layer of strategy. As a personal leadership dimension, Time Planning requires strong personal judgment and sales process expertise. It also requires some measure of autonomy over how a salesperson goes about allocating their time—more specifically, they need to be empowered to make trade-off calls in order to laser focus in on activities that drive revenue.

As an example, a salesperson might apply the strategic aspect of Time Planning to their own work by analyzing routine meetings and tasks to determine the opportunity costs associated with their continued involvement. Along those lines, there might be a standing Tuesday morning meeting that the salesperson has been attending for six months without getting much out of it. In that case, this individual might explain to their manager what it would look like if that time could be repurposed for the important work of tailoring a series of outreach messages to potential leads.

Now this application is contingent on a company's culture, specifically the spoken and unspoken rules of how things get done around there. Cultivating strong Time Planning in salespeople requires an internal environment where those who have developed a reputation for being highly capable can exercise decision-making and control over their timing without repercussion. Ideally, these salespeople would work with their managers on individual trade-off calls involving their time, knowing that there exists top-down support for implementing this important personal leadership strategy.

Time Planning has a few more distinguishable attributes and

activities that a salesperson can embed into their work stream. First is developing a habit that focuses on a next-logical-step method for all internal tasks and external opportunities. This is where process knowledge becomes so important. Salespeople cannot focus on next steps unless they know the order and priority of how things get done. When they do understand how things work, part of Time Planning involves keeping track of priority activities that require attention. Certain examples related to sales process might include researching a prospective client or company, preparing an agenda before each sales meeting, organizing client details, and maintaining records in a CRM. Other examples related to internal process and expectations might be preparing information or reports, pulling together client information to help inform a product development team, or participating in a relevant training event. When a salesperson breaks down their work stream into specific activities, they are able to use Time Planning to thoughtfully allocate their time to each area based on priority level.

Contrast this proactive approach with a much more common passive approach to time. When salespeople are more passive, those prior examples are still swirling around the work stream—there is just no order or logic in play to make sense of it. What happens next is predictable. A passive approach to everyday work leads to procrastination and firefighting. The salesperson has forfeited control over their day and is forced to work reactively.

Time Planning offers a different reality. When practiced consistently, a salesperson takes command of their calendar. They work to set goals based on the best potential for productivity and then assign tasks accordingly. Now armed with this priority set of tasks, a salesperson goes into resource management mode. They will analyze their calendar and determine how they can trade their valuable blocks of time for work on activities that will translate directly or indirectly to revenue.

This practice also includes a salesperson building in margins into their day to deal with the inevitable urgent or reactive tasks that creep up. In other words, to fight fires. However, that simple step of building in margin creates the necessary space to keep potential fires from consuming more of their time resources than they should. Finally, as salespeople achieve fluency in Time Planning, they will recognize the importance of communicating their time plan internally to others. When a salesperson's manager and colleagues understand the how and the why behind a salesperson's time plan, it increases the odds that the plan will be respected and have staying power. At the very least, if trade-off calls have to be made, the existence of an established time plan will surely provoke the right internal conversations.

THREE WATCHOUTS

1. Allowing someone else's needs or other external factors to drive how work time is spent and deferring other things that deserve greater prioritization
2. Stopping short of breaking down a client relationship or account sales strategy into progressive daily, weekly, and monthly tasks
3. Getting easily distracted by new possibilities or exciting outcomes that can replace the extended task focus required to advance potentially less interesting opportunities

Given how observable Time Planning is when it is put into practice, any related watchouts would likewise also most likely be observable. One of the most common time-related challenges happens with salespeople who struggle with the fundamentals. More specifically, they struggle with *allowing someone else's needs or other external factors to drive how work time is spent and deferring other things that deserve greater prioritization.* It is not difficult to identify this watchout in play on your sales team. If a seller operates in this way, chances are they have gained a reputation as someone who struggles to manage their time. Two common factors contribute to this behavior pattern. First, when a salesperson approaches their time this way, it may be because they lack insight or knowledge into what activities need to be managed in order to achieve their goals. Possessing an incomplete scope of required activities can trigger a cycle of reactivity. When something pops up that a salesperson didn't anticipate or plan for, it has a downstream effect. In all likelihood, what a salesperson had hoped to accomplish in a given day gets pushed off until after they've dealt with a surprise fire. Then, by the time the salesperson turns their attention back to the activities they were originally trying to accomplish, it's quite possible that the delay has now made that more urgent. As this reactive cycle continues, the salesperson creates a greater time deficit for themselves. After this becomes the norm, a salesperson may feel like their ability to exert any control over their calendars has at best become confusing and at worst feels impossible.

Another contributing factor is a salesperson's struggle to erect and enforce boundaries. This is especially common with sellers who have friendly and accommodating personalities. The challenge is that while these individuals have the best intentions, they struggle to factor in opportunity cost. Each time they say yes to someone or something that doesn't somehow connect to generating revenue, they are costing themselves and the company money. Oftentimes these contributing factors go hand in hand. When a salesperson doesn't draw a line between the important things that advance their sales goals and the less relevant activities, they waste valuable time.

There are always those individuals who do a good enough job managing their time. They aren't squeezing all they can out of every workday, but their hair isn't always on fire either. If you were to ask these salespeople to share some detail around their methods, what you'd likely discover is that they don't have a formal plan. Instead, these salespeople take a commonsense approach to managing their time. This can work for a while, but when a salesperson starts feeling the crunch of needing to accelerate their activity to meet looming goals, more aggressive methods are required. Salespeople who manage their time more casually are unfortunately often *stopping short of breaking down a client relationship or account sales strategy into progressive daily, weekly, and monthly tasks.* Without this added rigor, a salesperson is still primarily operating in a tactical zone. This is common without a true working knowledge of sales process. Without this understanding, it's much more difficult for salespeople to translate account strategy into activities and tasks—a capability that is critical for effective Time Planning.

Sales process also helps salespeople recognize what stage their deal is in, based on how the client is behaving. This clarity helps a salesperson allocate their time toward the strategic activities that will establish a chain of progression and momentum with their clients. When salespeople have less clarity, they usually take a deadline- or urgency-driven approach to working with clients. Add to this any tendency toward procrastination, and time deficits start compounding quickly. This is when we start getting 11:00 p.m. emails from salespeople catching up on the work that piled up throughout the day.

The crime of this last watchout emerges when salespeople are pursuing new and fun things. On a lighter note, we might also call this issue seller Kryptonite. Consider what happens when a salesperson struggles with *getting easily distracted by new possibilities or exciting outcomes that can replace the extended task focus required to advance potentially less interesting opportunities.* This is sometimes referred to as chasing shiny objects. At first, the tendency may be harmless, but the more this habit occurs, the more devastating it is at eroding the salesperson's time.

There is nothing wrong with exciting new opportunities. If marketing provides some promising new logos fresh off a campaign, you want your salespeople primed and enthusiastic to engage. Similarly, if you tap them on the shoulder and want them to deliver a main-stage presentation at your sales kickoff to highlight their successful sales tactics, you want them to take this invitation seriously. The problem is that when a salesperson hasn't strategically allocated their time, they don't have visibility into what they are pushing off in favor of this new thing that has captured their attention. Salespeople who do this are more likely to allow their feelings and impulses to dictate the way they work.

The more successful a salesperson is, the more is at stake when they're cavalier with their time. Most of the best client wins require dedicated work each day in the trenches. Choosing to pursue something fun over an extended task focus can have all sorts of consequences—not the least of which is the end-of-quarter or end-of-year blitz when the salesperson tries to apply added pressure to move deals along rather than being disciplined about using their time daily to achieve progress gradually.

THREE BELIEFS

1. Time is your most precious resource.
2. Balance distractions with boundaries.
3. Sharing your approach to Time Planning makes it real.

Of course, the life of a salesperson need not be an all-tedious-work-and-no-play proposition. Time Planning is the practice that gives back. When salespeople use Time Planning principles wisely and build margin into their day, they end up having *more* flexibility to fight fires or indulge in fun new things. The difference is that valuable and finite blocks of time have been strategically allocated in advance. Time Planning also has a salesperson putting the necessary boundaries into place to know when someone or something has started encroaching on their time. When this happens, they have established open lines of communication for working with their manager on trade-off calls. This discipline, like all others, is rooted in a strong belief system—in this case, it is related to time.

The foundational belief is about recognizing that *time is your most precious resource.* While this is rather straightforward and easy to remember, putting it into practice requires focus. Salespeople must create a system of prioritization around their client accounts that covers preparation, client interaction, documentation, internal responsibilities, and margin—which again are blocks of working time that can be repurposed to deal with unexpected issues.

A popular personal finance concept is zero-based budgeting. This philosophy involves total allocation of monthly dollars. All savings and expenditures are subtracted from monthly income until the earner is zeroed out. This intentionality ensures that each dollar is earmarked to pay down obligations and advance wealth objectives. This same philosophy can work with time. Call it zero-based Time Planning. In this case, every block of every day is allocated intentionally toward revenue priorities, with margin time being used for the extras or fires. Establishing habits like this is especially important when you consider that while an individual can theoretically always earn more money, they cannot manufacture more time.

This next belief goes a bit further than the first. If time is our most precious resource, then salespeople have to recognize how important it is to *balance distractions with boundaries.*

Not to be too dramatic, but given how limited time is, salespeople have to take up practical ways to defend it like their success depends on it—because it does. When a new shiny object presents itself, it can be very tempting to push aside existing plans and focus on things that appear to produce a quick reward. However, it is possible to both explore new things *and* stay on track with other priorities. It starts with effective use of boundaries. When a salesperson does this well, they will expend their margin time—call it two hours—on something new that has come up. When that time has elapsed, the salesperson will recognize that they are at a boundary point. Rather than allowing the fun or excitement to spill over "just fifteen more minutes," they will put a pin in it for the day and move on to what's been scheduled next. If more time *must* be used, they might borrow it from tomorrow's margin, but the key is continued exertion of control of their schedule—never allowing any one thing to get too out of hand. This put-and-take approach helps strengthen both Time Planning and Personal Ownership capabilities as salespeople become more aware and more disciplined around counting the costs of their decisions.

Finally, salespeople should believe that *sharing your approach to Time Planning makes it real.* This belief supports efforts to set boundaries and preserve time. When taking a proactive approach to Time Planning and establishing a system of prioritization, it is important for salespeople to share their methods and thinking with others. The salesperson's first discussion should always be with their direct manager to get buy-in and support for the what and the why behind the Time Planning approach.

Next, the salesperson should communicate their approach to other close colleagues and internal team managers. This effort to include and inform others makes it easier when a salesperson may have to be an optional attendee at a standing meeting or might need to decline a nonurgent request so that there is an awareness for why the salesperson may need to be an optional attendee or may not be able to take on another request. While sales leaders may need to, at times, put their own boundaries around a salesperson's boundary setting for business reasons, it is important to work together and create the right environment that encourages and supports salespeople in taking their time seriously.

Chapter 10

Service Mindset

Creates high levels of satisfaction by demonstrating interest and care for the service needs of others, bringing the right resources to bear, and putting personal energy behind creating consistently positive experiences that drive loyalty over time.

Thirty years ago, excellent service was a bona fide differentiator for businesses that were willing to make it a significant pillar in their strategy. Remember these near-antiquated words: *The customer is always right.* Certain retail stores became known for gladly accepting all kinds of returns, no questions asked. Others would go out of their way to ensure that a custom order was handled with care and delivered to a buyer's exact specifications. As a consumer, chances are you loved how it felt to be the beneficiary of this spectacular service. Perhaps you told others about your experience, or you just remained loyal to that business because they made you feel valued. For a long time, this was the norm—customers expected and enjoyed great service.

As business started changing, placing greater emphasis on technology, this service culture began to suffer. Of course, technology is a wonderful thing. It has allowed companies to grow, scale, and reduce costs. It has afforded consumers more access and, when it works, ease of use. However, what we've seen play out is a cause-and-effect-type relationship between technology and service. As technology's star kept rising, service faded at an equally rapid pace. The challenge with service is that it is inherently personal. So the more technology has taken people out of the equation, the more customer experience has suffered. Growing companies are starting to take notice of this service deficit, and many are having some serious conversations about how it can once again become a pillar of business strategy.

One example of this is the prevalence of the Customer Success (CS) role. The need for this type of position was born out of the software as a service (SaaS) segment and has been adopted in some form or another by nontech companies whose business models also depend on customer renewals. The general concept behind CS is to assign individuals who would walk with the customer during solution implementation and in the weeks and months that follow to ensure that they have the knowledge, skills, and resources to use what they bought on a regular basis within their business. Naturally, if a customer utilizes a product or service regularly, a contract renewal should be all but guaranteed.

However, in reality, this approach doesn't go far enough to address how a customer feels about doing business with the organization, meaning that their loyalty is not in any way assured. Enter in the concept of Customer Experience (CX). Advocates for CX recognize that focusing on product or service utilization no longer goes far enough to create any sort of competitive advantage.

The speed of innovation in recent years has meant that one company could come out with a new concept one minute and before long could be dealing with a whole host of copycat competitors all trying to grab at market share. These me-too solutions often differentiate themselves with a more attractive price and perhaps an expanded feature set. Before long, early existing users and new prospective customers have several options from which to choose. Many of these organizations have been deciding to challenge themselves toward creating a CX strategy that will strengthen customer impressions. When a great experience is paired with a great product and a great price, these business leaders are banking on this triple threat to serve as their distinct competitive advantage. In other words, in large part these companies are betting on service once again.

Salespeople are a major component of full-scale experience initiatives or even a CX lite. The challenge remains that since service focus has taken a back seat in our modern business environments, our sales teams have become deconditioned in this area. It is not uncommon for them to be polite with clients and provide a good sales experience to close a deal, all the while truly believing that service is someone else's job. To reverse this outlook and recondition salespeople to participate in delivering consistent customer experiences, we look to Service Mindset. This dimension and its associated behaviors can act as a blueprint for helping sellers understand their service role with the context of relationship-based selling.

THREE WATCHOUTS

1. Treating nonsales-related client issues with less interest, perhaps asking one or two questions but stopping short of digging for root cause
2. Poorly executing handoffs to other colleagues, creating an inconsistent experience for clients
3. Not logging, communicating, or tracking the resolution of expressed service issues, risking a negative impact to the overall client relationship strategy

When service isn't something that a business consistently monitors, people can gradually develop apathy in this area. The more widespread this is within an organization, the more challenging it is to tackle. As it relates to the sales team, some more specific signs and indicators can be easier to recognize and ultimately address through a renewed belief system.

The three Service Mindset watchouts are related to each other and, when taken together, form a chain of service dysfunction. Salespeople who lack a Service Mindset run the risk of *treating nonsales-related client issues with less interest, perhaps asking one or two questions but stopping short of digging for root cause.* In most cases, if a salesperson thinks that offering some service will eventually lead to a closed deal, there may be some temporary motivation to go above and beyond. For example, let's say that a good prospect requests a company white paper that was released last year. In that case, the salesperson will more likely than not add it to their task list, pull the resource, write a friendly message, and send it over to the client. They might even offer to walk the client through the highlights of the white paper over the phone. We can essentially define this as transactional service, which occurs when a salesperson's service efforts are applied only to active deals.

However, when service is applied situationally like this, it creates inconsistency in the customer experience. Salespeople with this watchout may provide great care and attention during the sales cycle and then, post-sales, the client feels a noticeable cooling off. As another example, a salesperson might lavish attention on what they think is a hot lead. However, if after a few exchanges the salesperson realizes that the prospective customer is interested but now is not the right time for them to buy, the salesperson may not hide their efforts to quickly disengage or hand them off. How is that future customer going to feel about that salesperson and their company when the time does become right to buy?

At the core of these two illustrations are salespeople who assign service importance according to immediate sales probability only.

The next link in the service dysfunction chain involves *poorly executing handoffs to other colleagues, creating an inconsistent experience for clients.* The more teams your company has that engage with your customers, the more pervasive this second watchout might be with your sellers. When a salesperson is concerned only with the immediate service that they personally have to provide to advance a deal, they may be all too happy to push the remaining responsibility around customer experience onto other internal teams—and point to others if things go off the rails.

One visual way to describe this behavior is the tendency to fling things over the wall. These sloppy handoffs can happen as a salesperson pushes an opportunity or client over to platform demonstrations, support or operations, contracts and billing, implementation, training, or CS. It's usually done with incomplete or missing information, and when these departments attempt to engage with the client, the experience can feel like retracing old steps and be incredibly frustrating. For example, let's say that during discovery, a client shared with the salesperson at an SaaS company their specific use case and why they were evaluating the product. Now let's say that the salesperson offered to arrange a platform demo with the client (transactional service). However, what the salesperson actually did was just reach out to the scheduler and put both parties in touch so that they could find a mutually agreeable time to meet for the demo. The salesperson did not take the time to provide client background, insights, use cases, or suggested flow to the demonstration specialist. Now, when the client signs on, the demonstration specialist just does what they always do—presents a generic rundown of features and benefits in no particular order. Lacking any connection to their business, the client struggles to understand how these features work to support the specific way that they want to use the product. Sensing the disconnect, the salesperson takes themselves off mute and in real time jumps in and starts directing the demonstration specialist on where to navigate in the drop-down menu or where to click. The client walks away from this experience confused and annoyed.

The third watchout and final link in this service dysfunction chain occurs when a salesperson makes a habit of *not logging, communicating, or tracking the resolution of expressed service issues, risking a negative impact to the overall client relationship strategy*. We covered transactional service and poor handoffs with the first two Service Mindset obstacles. This third one completes the picture. When a salesperson doesn't recognize the importance of client experience and the service undercurrent that runs beneath, they don't develop conscientious supporting behaviors.

The fallout from an inconsistent customer experience first and foremost impacts the salesperson—ignoring service cues can lead to revenue consequences. If another competitor gets the service equation right, and the salesperson or by association the salesperson's company gets it wrong, new deals may be jeopardized. If an existing client experiences low levels of service after the sale, their loyalty may be at stake, and the salesperson can eventually face attrition issues. The way a client perceives service is a critical lever of a seller's Growing Relationships strategy. The bottom line is that the service factor is either working for the salesperson or against them.

THREE BELIEFS

1. The gap between service expectations and actual client experience is *my* role.
2. Issues flung over the wall often land with a thud.
3. Consistent service can be linked to future revenue.

Helping salespeople develop their service muscle is part belief based and part cultural. If your organization has decided to focus on a CX strategy, no matter how robust or light, it should be clearly defined. This shift should also be communicated internally from the top down, including expectations and a path to recognition.

If exceptional service is already a part of your company's fabric, then this is an opportunity to fine-tune this capability throughout your sales team. Doing so will ratchet up consistency and ensure that it becomes a strong, competitive differentiator. The following series of beliefs can counteract a chain of service dysfunction and help people incrementally improve their behavior.

Salespeople have to believe that *the gap between service expectations and actual client experience is* my *role.* Often during the sales cycle, a seller will paint the best possible picture of what sort of service the client can expect from working with their company. This messaging gets etched into the client's mind, and each time an actual experience turns out to be opposite from what's promised, they notice. Some may even keep score, thinking that it creates some kind of relationship leverage. On the opposite end, if a salesperson doesn't set *any* service expectations, then the client defaults to their opinion of great service. As a result, they will establish their own ideas around what sort of service to expect.

When salespeople believe that client perceptions of service are their responsibility, then it becomes an agenda item for sales interactions. During discovery, as a salesperson is learning about the client's goals and priorities, they will also take the time to include the topic of service. They will message their company's capabilities accurately and upsell where premium services are offered. In other words, salespeople will take Personal Ownership over the service equation because they believe that it matters to the client and to their business. For those reasons, a service-minded seller will not leave matters of customer experience to chance.

The next belief confronts a common service-limiting behavior: *Issues flung over the wall often land with a thud.* Despite higher levels of Personal Ownership, many things still compete for a salesperson's time and attention. While it may not seem practical to give everything that comes up during the sales cycle the same care and attention, salespeople who have cultivated a Service Mindset tend to operate on the principle that if an issue matters to the client, it has to matter to them. These sellers also recognize that sloppy handoffs today create massive cleanup efforts tomorrow. So they tend to take the extra time to transfer issues well. Salespeople who have adopted this belief will also take the time to frame the situation and offer suggestions or advice to their colleagues on how to solve them. They will choose to stay involved, if only in the role of watchful observer. Service-minded salespeople do this because they want to stay informed and be well positioned to pick up the sales baton again after a matter has been resolved.

Finally, it's important to recognize that *consistent service can be linked to future revenue.* When salespeople internalize the reality that a strong service experience can lead to creating future paths to revenue, it places a greater importance on prioritizing service issues as they arise. They now seem less like nuisances and more like relationship-building opportunities.

As salespeople take an interest in their clients' service issues, they also gain added context and insights. The more knowledgeable a salesperson becomes about the root cause of service issues and the client's rationale behind their asks, the more they can apply those insights toward developing ways to grow the relationship in the future. As an example, if a salesperson learns that a larger client needs more resources around training and digs to find out more about what that looks like, they may be able to pass notes from their detailed discovery along internally as an idea for extending the company's support services. Assuming the company is open to making this investment, once the package is built, the salesperson could arrange a pilot with their client or identify that client as an early buyer of these expanded services. This win-win is only possible because the salesperson made it their business to connect the service dots.

When salespeople model consistent service, it provides a noticeable tailwind in the sales process and becomes a strong factor in any broader organizational effort to provide a robust customer experience.

Chapter 11

Winning Drive

Demonstrates the strong but controlled desire to achieve defined, successful outcomes and puts the right action and energy behind it by creating a game plan to relentlessly pursue and prioritize the most promising opportunities.

One thing nearly everyone in the sales profession recognizes is the link between a competitive nature and success. Salespeople love to win. Decades of research supports this notion as well. The fairly recent fascination with the concept of grit has grown in popularity because of its ability to describe some of the individual traits required to channel an inner competitiveness. In a nutshell, grit often results in supportive behaviors such as perseverance and endurance. However, just developing grit in salespeople alone isn't enough to produce consistent results. Grit, while compelling, is just the tip of the iceberg.

In some ways, the origins of grit lie in professional athletics. People are always fascinated by how these competitors combine sheer talent with dedication to win the biggest contests. Along these lines, the comparison between salespeople and athletes has become so commonplace that it's almost lost its impact as a helpful analogy. In reality, there are more differences than there are similarities between the two. Most athletes are inherently disciplined. They grind out their conditioning, agility, practice, and nutrition regimens day after day, year after year. For most salespeople, that level of practice and performance consistency remains an aspiration.

But perhaps one of the biggest differences between the two groups is the full recognition of the game they are playing and how best to align their behavior. A football player's competitive identity is rooted in football. Chances are you won't see a wide receiver skipping a team practice on running routes because they've decided it would be better for their game-day performance if they picked up a bat instead. Similarly, you wouldn't see a strong ice hockey prospect with the desire to move out and up from the farm system taking a pass on skating practice because they feel that dribbling a basketball is better suited to meet their goals. There just isn't this sort of editorialization in the athletic world. These competitors know their sport, and the elites know what it takes to win at the professional or Olympic level.

For many salespeople, this just isn't so. If your team has experienced salespeople on it, then prior to arriving at your organization, these sellers worked other places. Those past experiences created certain mindsets and learned behaviors that they've imported over to your company. Chances are your marketplace, ideal clients, business strategy, and game plan differ from the other companies that your sellers worked at previously. Yet salespeople often stick with what they know. In other words, they may very well agree with you that running routes is important, but when they're left to their own devices, you notice them off to the side swinging the baseball bat.

Your team may also have welcomed people who are newer to the sales role. Perhaps they have a natural competitive streak and tell you that they want to learn. As a leader, you are initially delighted by how driven to win they appear. However, as more time goes by, you find yourself starting to question what game they are playing. As you observe their behaviors and actions, it seems they don't understand your go-to-market plan, how your company makes money, what its value proposition is, or how to guide clients. At first glance it might seem like a training issue, but with further reflection it's actually not as much of a knowledge issue as it is an application issue. They want to win so badly that they aren't thinking critically or determining the best opportunities to pursue. These new salespeople seem to have a start-stop rhythm going with their efforts to grow and develop. They sporadically apply the practices they've been taught, falling back on feeling or intuition to justify behaviors.

The good news is that, like many performance challenges, both types of behavioral issues can be resolved through performance coaching. With seasoned sellers, those coaching conversations become more about reconditioning old mindsets and habits so that they can perform best with your clients in your environment. For newer salespeople, coaching becomes more about clarifying knowledge and applying best practices with consistency to the highest potential client opportunities. These coaching conversations can use the Winning Drive dimension as a baseline to develop both seasoned and new salespeople alike.

Winning Drive defines what sales competitiveness looks like when it is fully matured and well harnessed. The dimension combines elements of grit and mental toughness with application of the salesperson to everyday work. Winning Drive behaviors help to shape and channel a salesperson's innate desire to win so that it accomplishes revenue goals. As you develop this dimension across the sales team, it elevates the importance of discipline and endurance as a way to achieve long-term success on your field of play.

THREE WATCHOUTS

1. Pursuing activity without a complete understanding of business context, strategy, solution value, incentive plans, or process
2. Self-directing sales efforts based largely on feelings and intuition
3. Fighting against the grain or passively resisting established order, resulting in battles or skirmishes that can deplete energy and time reserves

Having reviewed some of the macro-level obstacles that contribute to underdeveloped Winning Drive in salespeople, let's consider three common watchouts to add a little more color. First, let's drill down on what it looks like when salespeople are *pursuing activity without a complete understanding of business context, strategy, solution value, incentive plans, or process.* Sometimes we associate the phrase "Ready, fire, aim!" with this sort of behavior. These salespeople tend to operate in go mode, seemingly ready to pounce on whatever opportunity seems viable. They focus on clients who appear ready to buy without connecting the dots on the viability of this client or the opportunity. In other words, they don't take a step back to analyze whether a prospective client has a need that fits with what their business can solve for—and profitably.

This watchout is in force for salespeople who have become comfortable operating with just enough knowledge and information to get by. These sellers are often self-confident (perhaps overconfident) and have an inner, restless desire to win. They lean heavily on their own perceived talent to pull in as many deals as possible, the quality of those deals notwithstanding. Of course, over time this method does not serve the business or the salesperson well. In fact, as a company's sales strategy and incentive plans change to meet shifts in the market, these sellers are some of the slowest and most stubborn to embrace change.

Similarly, the next watchout is in play when a salesperson is *self-directing sales efforts based largely on feelings and intuition.* Businesses that lack a defined sales process with common understanding and language make it much easier for this behavior to go undetected. By nature, an established objective sales process serves as a check on feelings or intuition.

Overall, this watchout tends to have some staying power. While salesperson instincts are valuable, when those instincts are given disproportionate weight to make no-go or go-forward decisions, it becomes a problem. Sellers who rely heavily on their feelings and intuition to direct their pursuits and sales efforts will regularly have inaccurate pipelines. They will call lukewarm leads qualified prospects and will rate sales opportunities as further along in the process than they really are. These bad inputs result in poor outputs. When salespeople and sales leaders are working with bad data, it compromises the ability to accurately forecast and track activity.

The final watchout illustrates what it looks like when a salesperson's innate competitiveness becomes aggression. In these cases, a seller may be *fighting against the grain or passively resisting established order, resulting in battles or skirmishes that can deplete energy and time reserves.* There is a fine line between being assertive and being aggressive. The former requires an unrelenting focus, whereas the latter may spill over into confrontation or even misconduct. A telltale sign of a salesperson struggling with this issue is one who engages in knife fights or skirmishes with their colleagues to get their own way.

On the client side, a salesperson might ignore the wishes of a primary contact and sidestep that individual if they believe that they can gain access to and ultimately win with someone higher up the ladder who they feel is more important. Related to both of these examples, a particularly wise sales coach once said, "If you operate like a hammer, then everything around you looks like a nail, so you keep swinging." That may be the best way to describe salespeople with these habits. The desire to get their own way manifests itself in a type of warfare that looks like creating conflict, wearing others down, manipulating circumstances, and other counterproductive behaviors. Given that in extreme cases this watchout can border on harassing or bullying behavior, it may ultimately require human resources (HR) intervention. However, for minor or incidental occurrences, individual coaching can bring awareness and behavior change.

THREE BELIEFS

1. Knowledge accelerates winning.
2. Objective client behavior is the best success predictor.
3. Winners are always advancing.

Standing in direct contrast to the first watchout is our first belief: *Knowledge accelerates winning.* The more a salesperson understands their role and how things are designed to function at their company and on their team, the better informed their actions will become. They will be able to harness their talent and competitive drive to win well.

How much access do salespeople have to the CEO at your company? These chief executives are often tapped to lead growing organizations because of their strong grasp of the market and how to gain share. Many can beautifully articulate the landscape, challenges, competitors, and where their companies fit in—and they most certainly know how the business makes its money. Apart from, say, an annual kickoff meeting appearance, perhaps a practical way to help salespeople become more knowledgeable is to arrange for them to learn more from your CEO. Think about how they might benefit from hearing this individual articulate and reinforce the basics of that message on a regular basis. Certainly, a live delivery is better than a recorded version. This additional effort would demonstrate leadership's investment in the success of its sales team and help salespeople increase their strategic knowledge of the business, making it easier to achieve the right outcomes.

The next belief in the Winning Drive series relates to daily application of sales process in your organization. Believing that *objective client behavior is the best success predictor* helps balance tendencies toward relying on feelings and instincts to rate deal probability.

A strong sales process includes progressive stages and customer indicators along the way to help sellers grade their opportunities according to a defined standard. While a salesperson may have a good feeling about a prospect, if they cannot be objectively qualified by, say, confirming budget availability for a potential purchase or that they have priority needs that are creating urgency, then that salesperson would weight this real client evidence over their instincts. They would rate the deal accordingly. Repeating this practice with every lead and across their assigned accounts would create strong pipelines and ensure that salespeople are allocating their time toward the strongest opportunities to increase their win rate.

The final belief exists to more precisely define what competitive salespeople already know, which is that *winners are always advancing*. However, in this case advancement must be tied closely to the company's business strategy. Leaning into other dimensions such as Growing Relationships and Time Planning, this Winning Drive belief guides a salesperson toward approaching their assigned accounts both strategically and systematically. To chart an advancement course, a salesperson might begin with their annual sales goal and then identify three achievable goals at the assigned account level to accomplish this quarter. Salespeople can keep themselves on track by setting an ongoing calendar block to review progress against these goals and advance next logical steps.

After working this way at the assigned account level, a seller can go a little more granular and repeat this same method at the opportunity level. In this case, they would segment opportunities with the greatest revenue potential for more precise goal planning. This type of habit building puts structures and systems around a salesperson's innate competitiveness and ensures that they are taking the right steps forward in alignment with the rules of your game and the best interests of the business.

Chapter 12

Inner Resolve

Remains emotionally composed and projects strength in the face of conflict and setbacks, leveraging internal optimism and a balanced view of circumstances to logically navigate stress, pressure, demands, or challenges.

As much as we want to shape and channel competitiveness in salespeople, it is equally important to ensure that they are resilient and adaptive. As the world continues to evolve at warp speed, salespeople must develop a new level of inner strength to serve as a stabilizing force through bouts of trial and change. To help salespeople meet this challenge, the Inner Resolve dimension sits at the anchor position as the last of the five personal leadership capabilities.

Inner Resolve doesn't just help salespeople hunker down and try to survive setbacks or failures. Instead, it helps them lean into challenging times and learn valuable lessons they can apply toward similar experiences in the future. That isn't to say that salespeople won't experience emotional stress during trying times. They absolutely will. However, Inner Resolve helps people make sense of what's happening around them in the healthiest way possible. It equips them to recognize external or internal stress triggers, rationalize them, respond well, and draw insight from the outcomes.

Cultivating Inner Resolve across your sales team creates the sort of resiliency that produces more steady and reliable performance results over time. When choosing to make this important dimension a development opportunity for the sales team, it is helpful to be aware that not everyone may be eager to discuss triggers in the workplace.

Originally, talk of triggers was more likely to be explored within a clinical context. Within that environment, the term *triggers* has been most commonly associated with serious conditions such as posttraumatic stress disorder. Recognizing the situations or circumstances that can become catalysts for distress remains an important part of professional therapy. However, more recently the concept of triggers has taken on a broader meaning. Now when people talk about triggers, they may be referring to something in everyday life that sets off negative emotions in someone.

Take, for instance, two people in a heated confrontation. Let's say that during this war of words, one person upsets the other through their nonverbal mannerisms. Maybe it was an eye roll or finger-pointing. In this situation, asserting that a person's behavior is a trigger for the aggrieved party is ideally supposed to create some explicit social pressure that causes the antagonist in this case to back off. The downside of this fairly new interpersonal dynamic is that the aggrieved party is substituting social pressure for their own ability to confront the trigger and work through it using more sophisticated coping skills. In other words, this easy-to-implement defense strategy doesn't cultivate resiliency and actually does people harm in the long run.

Within the workplace environment, and especially with clients, sophisticated coping skills are essential. It's important to find healthy mindsets and habits that are helpful in working through the things that challenge our emotions.

In most businesses, it would not be appropriate for a salesperson to assertively confront a client for leveling constructive criticism that may be hard to hear. Nor would it be productive to take the pushback so personally that it becomes incredibly difficult for the salesperson to rebound and refocus. With this in mind, it is beneficial for sales leaders to set expectations that external and internal stress triggers are inevitable. It is equally important for these leaders to help their sales team grow in the area of resiliency. Inner Resolve provides the way forward. This Diligence Dimension can be applied in the most practical sense to help salespeople who are working on their ability to cope with stressors to deal with setbacks and disappointments. Doing this consistently well when the emotions are high and the stakes are higher is critical.

THREE WATCHOUTS

1. Operating without a recognition of workplace triggers and without effective coping strategies to manage them
2. Allowing elevated emotions, potentially self-characterized as passion, to overtake facts, logic, or practical steps forward
3. Placing extended focus on uncontrollable circumstances without acknowledging and acting on factors that are controllable

Just like some of the other personal leadership dimensions we've covered, Inner Resolve and related concepts such as stress triggers and emotionality are inherently personal. While many of the other Diligent Framework dimensions are primarily shaped by various workplace experiences, the way that a person reacts to challenging circumstances could be traced as far back as early childhood. For that reason, a wide range of watchouts can hinder progress in this area. Given the personal nature of this subject matter, it is best to explore any related watchouts with individual salespeople in private settings during one-on-one coaching. Even though different people may have different obstacles to operating with high levels of Inner Resolve, there are a few common areas on which to focus.

While it isn't difficult for most people to recognize when negative feelings creep in, many are nevertheless *operating without a recognition of workplace triggers and without effective coping strategies to manage them.* In the most basic terms, sellers with lower levels of Inner Resolve are unable to properly define and make sense of certain types of situations and stressors. In the field of psychology, an important concept called attribution theory considers the ways that people take in, interpret, and draw conclusions about situations. For example, if something good happens, like a difficult deal has finally closed, a salesperson can process that experience as either situational or enduring. In other words, the closed deal was either luck or it was destiny. On the flip side, if that same deal was lost, the salesperson could either attribute that loss to themselves personally or they could depersonalize it, perceiving the outcome as more coincidental—perhaps it just wasn't the right time for the client.

Individual perceptions and stress triggers are deeply intertwined. How a salesperson views a particular situation will determine how impactful an associated trigger is or is not. Within the workplace, there are five common pain points that will generate these individual perceptions and perhaps become triggers for some people. These pain points include potential threats to a person's

- status;
- certainty or safety;
- autonomy;
- relationships; and
- equity or fairness.

Status is big for some salespeople—it speaks to positional power. A seller who has earned top-producer status may want internal recognition for their efforts. They may also want to be viewed as indispensable to their highest-revenue-producing accounts. Certainty or safety is about assurance, the maintaining of a steady or certain state. Of course, more serious matters of psychological or physical safety are nested under this category as well. However, this is most often about desiring certainty for everyday working conditions. As an example, many salespeople will say that maintaining an autonomous environment is critical to producing their best work, which is why the idea of getting a new boss can be a real stress trigger. When there's a new sheriff in town, people worry about their positional power, the certainty of their job, and the possibility that their working arrangement will diminish or perhaps they will be micromanaged. Relationships speak to factors like trust, quality, and shared views while equity or fairness are about seeing the right thing happen.

When salespeople aren't skilled at understanding their own perceptions and don't recognize which of the five pain points impact them the most, they will struggle with various aspects of emotional control. When this happens, salespeople may react by *allowing elevated emotions, potentially self-characterized as passion, to overtake facts, logic, or practical steps forward.*

When people ignore, justify, or excuse away strong emotional reactions, things get fuzzy. As stress triggers go undetected and unchecked, they start distorting the salesperson's view of the situation and complicating their work. In this elevated emotional state, feelings can overtake logic or facts and make it much harder for a salesperson to decide and determine their next steps forward.

The more vicious this cycle, the more truth (facts, logic, counternarrative) becomes the enemy of emotion (entrenched personal feelings). This watchout not only has a negative effect to the health and well-being of the individual salesperson but also can quickly spill over and impact the harmony and cohesion of the sales team. When emotions run high and things get distorted, it is often an invitation for negativity to seep in. When this happens, you risk a salesperson *placing extended focus on uncontrollable circumstances without acknowledging and acting on factors that are controllable.*

The more a person yields to an onslaught of negative emotions, the easier it is to get stuck in a mental rut. When a salesperson dwells on what's going wrong with a client or on things they cannot control for an extended period of time, it becomes very hard to turn the corner behaviorally. Negative thinking is the gateway to all sorts of issues. It even sneaks into more benign situations like being overwhelmed, which on the spectrum of conflict is certainly on the lower end. Yet if a salesperson is prone to negative self-talk like "I'll never be able to clear my plate or get out from under this pile of work," then even this can trigger a spiral of negativity. Explore this watchout through coaching. In these settings, it is important to encourage salespeople to focus on the things that they can control over what they cannot. While this continued reminder is simple advice, it is profoundly helpful.

THREE BELIEFS

1. Circumstances—good, bad, and in between—are temporary.
2. A personalized coping strategy empowers you to manage work triggers.
3. Challenges and setbacks teach the most memorable lessons.

Counteracting the power of emotions and developing an inner stability starts with the right mindset. With patience and commitment, it is possible for salespeople to reverse old ways of thinking and form healthy perceptions. The first in a series of Inner Resolve beliefs is about accepting that *circumstances—good, bad, and in between—are temporary.* This belief calls for salespeople to internalize the constant change that comes with this profession. It is also a call to live above everyday circumstances to become more purpose driven about their work. This approach helps to cultivate gratitude when good things happen and enduring patience in the midst of setbacks and trials. This broader view of work inherently diminishes the impact of bad circumstances. Let's say that a salesperson has made it their mission to use their company's solutions and personal expertise to add value and educate clients. In this case, when a promising deal ends up going to a competitor, they will seek feedback and then hunt down the next opportunity to help someone.

A personalized coping strategy empowers you to manage work triggers. Given the various types of personalities and how fluid things are in the workplace, not to mention with clients, facing potential stress triggers is inevitable. Reacting to these triggers can range from the nuisance of lingering thoughts that make it hard to be productive to feelings of frustration, anger, and an urge to act. This second belief is critical for empowering a salesperson to gain healthy emotional control over those triggers. It begins with understanding the interplay among perceptions, triggers, emotions, and behaviors. Then it requires doing some heavy lifting to become more aware of which triggers can provoke a reaction. This often involves some reflection and journaling around instances, big or small, that produce heightened emotion—this is known in therapeutic settings as metacognitive work.

Once a seller does the work of narrowing down what triggers can really impact them, they must personalize a coping strategy to manage those reactions. This could involve a regimen of positive self-talk or a mindfulness type of activity that brings on a sense of calm. It could also be a set of practices such as not emailing or instant messaging when in an emotional state. With time, practice, and coaching, salespeople can forge new patterns of thinking and behavior that are activated upon the first inkling of elevated emotions.

Challenges and setbacks teach the most memorable lessons. Perhaps the best aspect of Inner Resolve is its emphasis on applied learning. When salespeople are able to extract and apply lessons from painful experiences or extreme change, it is like a personal return on investment. Consider a rubber band. While its function is to stretch, when quickly released, there is a spring and an audible snap as it bounces back. With the right mindset, recognition, and coping strategies, salespeople can be as resilient, bouncing back quickly from all manner of challenges with that proverbial spring in their step. The speed and ease with which that happens is directly connected to their ability to internalize well-earned lessons and apply them to future circumstances.

When Inner Resolve is integrated into a sales team, the capability helps them become consistently productive and resilient over time. It aids sellers to process various experiences, control and channel emotions, apply valuable lessons learned, and work with greater adaptability. As teams reach a mastery level of Inner Resolve, they won't need the aggressive change management efforts they once did to cope with new realities. Instead, they will be ready and equipped to recognize, rationalize, and internalize the need for change and remain positive about what it means for their futures.

Part 3

Implementing Sales Effectiveness

Chapter 13

Leading with Diligence

The idea of an entire sales team practicing the ten Diligence Dimensions covered in the prior chapters with consistency may seem aspirational. However, with strategic implementation, it is entirely attainable.

As sales leaders weave each of these dimensions throughout the everyday work stream, habits will begin to form, and with time, those habits will start producing incrementally positive results. With even more time and sustained effort, this campaign of creating a common language and shared expectations will become that all-important, overarching umbrella for driving consistency across the sales function. This synchronization will also fully support sales leadership's efforts around territory, targets, and tracking and—ultimately—the overall success of the sales plan.

With this payoff in mind, let's briefly review some of the key concepts we've covered up to this point. Sales leaders can prepare their sales team to meet increasing demands for growth by doing the following:

- Leveraging a well-researched framework to serve as a North Star, driving a common approach, language, and expectations across the team

- Recognizing and breaking through common watchouts and critical beliefs associated with each Diligence Dimension to pave the way for the next level of sales performance
- Identifying and addressing problematic salesperson behavior as well as inconsistent practices within the sales function itself

Making these concepts actionable requires some important legwork for sales leaders. The first out-of-the-gate objective is to lay the groundwork for a strong sales effectiveness foundation within your organization. For some, this means moving away from the more informal ad hoc approach that worked fine during the earlier stages of your company's growth story—effective immediately. Or maybe your team has placed some focus on sales effectiveness already, but now is the chance to level up the approach—to smooth out the edges, connect the dots, and get the salespeople positioned to reach a higher level of performance. The sales effectiveness foundation will start with a connected vision and then layer in the three critical pillars of methodology, process, and a plan for development.

Of course, as with any change endeavor, it starts at the top as leadership's philosophies and behaviors evolve to meet the greater demands of the business. Without leadership buy-in and support, all this goes nowhere. This means you will have to do some things differently if you want your people to follow suit. Remember that salespeople will mimic what they see their leaders model, so it's critical for you to go first. Doing so says to the skeptics and critics on your team that you aren't introducing another idea du jour that is destined to flame out but rather that this new way is here to stay.

CONNECTED VISION

Leading with Diligence requires total clarity around the sales vision. When the sales team understands their roles within the broader business context, it changes everything. There is tremendous benefit to getting the top executive leader in your company in front of the team on a regular basis to articulate the story of your business—more specifically, the market landscape, challenges, competitors, and where your company sits among its competitors, including how the business makes its money. Remember that central belief of Winning Drive: *Knowledge accelerates winning*. Never underestimate the power of that moment when things click for a salesperson—it changes how they work.

Once that big picture clarity is set, it's time for sales leadership to pick up the baton. Now it's your turn to layer in the go-to-market plan in a way that emphasizes the why followed by territory, targets, and tracking. The bottom line of this exercise is to pull together and sequence the important information that will create clarity for the sales team. The reality is that many sales leaders assume that this clarity exists, but often it is far fuzzier at the individual salesperson level. So, ultimately, the goal is to connect the following points for the sales team:

- The story of your business
- The go-to-market plan
- The why
- Territory, targets, and tracking

When the team can see a clear link among a strong business vision, a compelling sales strategy, and their role in all of it, enthusiasm starts building. The more they are convinced and excited to be part of the equation, the more they pass that energy on to the clients they serve. This can be a key ingredient for you as a sales leader in developing your own secret sauce that moves your team forward at a faster pace. In other words, this positive inertia created by genuine connection to something bigger adds dimension and relevance to your tactical direction around territory, targets, and tracking.

If salespeople can't see the link among business vision, sales strategy, and role definition, it becomes very easy to lose sight of why the metrics (territory, targets, and tracking) even matter. You might also notice them improvising and assigning their own ideas to fill in the clarity gaps. Taking the steps to connect your sales vision to the broader purpose of the company goes a long way toward helping your salespeople maintain a higher-level view of the world.

MESSAGING MAKEOVER

Once this connected vision is in play, continual reinforcement and repetition are key. Take it from one particularly effective sales leader named Jim. He's been a sales team fixer of sorts for over thirty years and is especially big on using illustrations. Jim's approach is simple. He reduces every high-level concept down to a sketch or picture. If a message is multifaceted and requires understanding and buy-in, he strongly believes that it needs to be consolidated into a visual. As one example, Jim frequently sketched out the four primary decision points that buyers make during the sales process. He would scribble four boxes left to right on the back of a pad or whiteboard during a conversation and use the simple visual to ground whatever topic needed to be informed and influenced by how clients think.

This approach helps people at all levels (especially the higher ones) really understand important concepts in a way that doesn't overwhelm them or create boredom like slide decks, spreadsheets, or even lengthy verbal examples can often do. No doubt this is why we see so many infographics, explainer videos, and other highly visual marketing tools out there. This illustrative approach to storytelling works with prospective customers. This is why many companies are quick to invest in this mode of communication as part of their lead acquisition strategies.

The same method helps our internal colleagues and team members understand complex ideas or messages faster. Visual examples accelerate comprehension and recall quality. There are many marketing, operational, or even HR initiatives we could identify as ideal targets for this sort of visually persuasive messaging, though let's focus on the sales vision or your go-to-market plan for the moment—keeping in mind that the same idea can apply to any business function.

Chances are you have this year's approved sales plan contained within a slide deck or in a spreadsheet. Maybe you went through it in full or partially curated it for presentation at the annual sales kickoff meeting. Perhaps in doing so, the sales team responded enthusiastically with a collective optimism around the possibilities this year. However, in many sales organizations, that clarity and energy fades as the months and quarters tick by. The more distance between unveiling the plan early in the year and the present day, the more sales conversations start narrowing. They gradually become more myopic and focused on the tactics of—you guessed it—territory, targets, and tracking. As the aperture begins closing, the pressure to transact intensifies, and inconsistent sales behavior ensues.

The biblical book of Proverbs is full of sage, practical wisdom. Within the Common English Bible translation, Proverbs 29:18 begins with these relevant words, "Where there's no vision, the people get out of control." It's easy to appreciate the plainspokenness of the statement, as it wastes no time addressing the great power and reach of vision.

Realistically, vision casting and effectively messaging it is one of the core expectations we have of leaders. It is imperative to set a direction that will guide the organization's climb to the highest summits and peaks. So, after acknowledging the importance of vision, the passage issues a rather blunt and candid observation of what happens behaviorally when that big picture is lacking: People get out of control. Fortunately, most of us are not dealing with a runaway sales team that has broken down. However, consider this potential variance to the ancient text as application for our work in leading sales teams: *Lacking connection to the why, salespeople do their own thing*. As sales leaders, our goal is to use any and all methods of reinforcement to ensure that salespeople understand and apply the big picture vision to their work. Finding ways to communicate visually can go a long way toward creating memorable imprints for salespeople.

Another particularly strong revenue leader named John was able to do just that. He created a simple triangle sketch where each point represented three professional service organizations that each served the same profession from a slightly different angle. During conversations with other leaders or with salespeople, he would jump up, grab a marker, and sketch the visual while he was making his point. He'd move the marker over each organization as places the business needed to be inspired by, participate in, and ultimately leverage as a source for prospects—in that order. Each part of the triangle would also have two to three bullet points underneath that described in a bit more detail how the company was going to execute. He drew this illustration so many times in the various conference rooms throughout the building that you'd be hard pressed not to see a faint outline of it still visible on a newly erased whiteboard. In fact, there was some irony there—no matter what other conversations around advancing business would take place in those rooms, their best chance of success was being rooted in or traced back to the company's go-to-market strategy.

This simple but effective effort helps to orient salespeople and brings continual perspective to their work. It also helps to plug them into something bigger than territory, targets, tracking, or even just themselves.

SALES EFFECTIVENESS PROGRAM

Let's stick with illustrations for a moment and consider the image of a large planet. Imagine a Saturn-like planet with three rings encircling it. In this sketch, the planet itself is one of your company's prospective clients. Each of these potential relationships is operating within its own world, each with their own ecosystems and unique ways of doing things. In order to sell effectively into this client's world from an outsider's position, it is important to carefully align your process, people, and value propositions to what matters to them. This is often referred to as buyer-centered selling.

The three rings you can put into motion represent your company's Sales Methodology, Sales Process, and Sales Development Plan—all working in unison as a Sales Effectiveness Program. The rings all share the same track, with each having their own respective lanes that uniquely contribute to helping your company win. These sales effectiveness rings include the following:

- Sales Methodology: the principles and approach behind how your team sells
- Sales Process: a linear way to track the progression of individual opportunities
- Sales Development Plan: an outline of high performance and the approach toward building salesperson capabilities

In other words, Sales Methodology speaks to *how we sell* while Sales Process helps us *track our opportunities*, and sales development outlines *how we build capability in our people.* When these three components leverage common language and are woven together, they are especially powerful in bringing sales leadership and salespeople together. The Diligence Framework is the stabilizing force that runs through each of these components. These threads of consistency help you align critical sales behavior through every step and stage of your Sales Effectiveness Program.

SALES METHODOLOGY

Establishing how we sell is the first opportunity for sales leaders to either move from an ad hoc approach within their function or to level up consistency efforts. It helps to think of a Sales Methodology as a circle. At the very top of the circle is *confirm*. Here a salesperson works to verify a prospective client opportunity. Then, moving clockwise down the circle, the Sales Methodology continues progressing as it prompts the salesperson toward preparing for client discovery, where they will use questioning skills to *learn* about the client's situation. Using this new information, the salesperson and the client will exchange perspectives and *explore* possibilities. At the six o'clock position, the salesperson would formally *present* recommendations or solutions and then *engage* all manner of client feedback before moving into the official *close* at essentially the ten o'clock position on the circle. This repeatable cycle of confirm–learn–explore–present–engage–close is a good example of how a Sales Methodology guides salespeople to sell. In the next section, we'll look at how the Sales Process complements the methodology but offers a more granular, objective way of tracking specific sales opportunities.

Many sales leaders get their start with a formal Sales Methodology by licensing a proprietary offering from a consultant or sales training vendor. This appears to make sense because these providers have invested significant time and expertise into developing and fine-tuning their material. In turn, this promises to be a time-saver for a sales leader.

The downside to buying a Sales Methodology from a vendor is relevance and cost. Methodologies work only when they reflect how your organization needs its salespeople to sell to your clients. In order to have mass market appeal, most consultant or vendor methodologies are rather generic to start, but they often offer the option to customize them to better fit a particular business. This is where the cost factor comes into play, as providers typically require fees for both licensing and the customization of their generic content. These fees may be based on the number of users and may occur year over year. The vendor almost always retains ownership and control over the use of its intellectual property, even as you implement it into your organization.

Before you can determine what sort of Sales Methodology is best suited for your organization, you must identify the type of sale that best applies to your business. Generally speaking, there are four different types of outbound B2B sales:

1. Approach based
2. Solution/value based
3. Service based
4. Simplified sale

After you identify the sale type or mix of sale types that fit with how your organization needs to sell to its clients, then as a sales leader, you can build or source the right Sales Methodology. It is so important to never settle for something completely off the shelf. The confusion that comes with salespeople picking up on the gaps between what a generic methodology calls for versus what's actually required based on the sales type at *your* organization with *your* customers creates its own set of problems. Instead, focus on a Sales Methodology that tightly fits your requirements or one that offers a good structure with the flexibility to dial the focus up or down on various components to match the realities of your business. Ideally, your methodology should be able to grow with your company over time.

Once you have selected a Sales Methodology, it is important to roll it out well. So many best intentions fall short of their potential in the execution phase. Sales leaders should work with their managers, supervisors, coaches, trainers, and sales operations colleagues on a plan to integrate the methodology into the everyday work streams of their sales teams. As a side note, if you are licensing methodology content from a provider, be sure to review the contract for any limitations or considerations that could inform your implementation plan.

Ideally, look for ways to work the methodology language into your sales enablement resources. Ask managers to come back to the steps and language in their coaching conversations. The methodology needs to become part of your organization's fabric. Salespeople should understand not only your illustrative sales vision but also the type of sale that they engage in and the critical methodology steps that help them get traction with clients.

For example, if a company's sale type is Solution/Value, then chances are there is a lot of emphasis placed on the salesperson's ability to influence and persuade their clients. Of course, before they can even do that, it's important that they understand as much as possible about the client and the sales opportunity through Sales Methodology steps like learn and explore. So, while talking sales strategy with your team, go into more detail around the value component of your company's solution—ensuring that the salespeople really get it.

Then, as your management team focuses on everyday workflow and specific deals, place continued emphasis on helping salespeople excel during the selling steps, like learn and explore, where delivering value really matters. Each time a salesperson gets to these steps with a client, they should treat them as though they were neon lights. Managers can lean in and provide extra coaching and support with salespeople as they work with their clients to learn and explore. They can also tap into Diligence Dimensions like Securing Information and Persuasive

Communication to support learn and explore methodology steps as salespeople work to build rapport, uncover needs, and float ideas. Think of the Diligence Dimensions as the workhorse elements behind a Sales Methodology. The attention to watchouts, beliefs, and practices are the power source behind each component of the Sales Methodology.

SALES PROCESS

Sales Methodology and Sales Process share a familial relationship. While they possess similar DNA, their distinctive attributes make each of them equally required parts of a Sales Effectiveness Program. Two sides of the same coin, a Sales Methodology is more artful with its important milestones that define how sellers should engage with clients while the precision of a Sales Process is more about science.

A Sales Process is a beacon of objectivity in what can be a sea of sales subjectivity. It serves as a helpful reality check for sellers and sales leaders alike. A Sales Process and its stages are typically unique to an organization, but there are some common generalities across all B2B sales that, for discussion's sake, can be helpful when getting started.

It is important to clarify the difference between a Lead-Generation Process and a Sales Process. For organizations with defined marketing or business development/prospecting efforts, these activities require their own process. It is a preface of sorts to a Sales Process. Its function is to document and track the journey from when a prospect gains an awareness of a company to the earliest forms of engagement, which often include clicking on emails or filling out a form. Later forms of prospect engagement could be responding to a business development phone outreach. Processes that outline and document these early-stage activities may be called a Lead-Generation Process or a Marketing Funnel. This process would conclude with the production of a nearly qualified or fully qualified lead. That warm lead is handed off to a salesperson, thus triggering the start of the Sales Process journey.

A salesperson then pursues the marketing-qualified lead through the defined stages of the Sales Process, where it goes from a lead to a sales opportunity. So long as the client continues engaging with the salesperson in a progressive way, the Sales Process will help guide the salesperson as they verify, track, and advance their opportunities.

The stages of a Sales Process are typically numbered and begin with *fully qualifying* an opportunity, *discovery*, *solutioning*, and then continuing on through to *close* and likely *finalizing* the purchase. Diligence Dimensions can serve the Sales Process in the same way as they serve the Sales Methodology—as workhorse elements.

For example, if stage two of a Sales Process is discovery (the Sales Methodology steps of learn and explore), then Securing Information aligns nicely and guides a seller toward being well prepared, plumbing the depths for insights and filtering through information and CRM documentation. While the Sales Process provides specific, activity-based direction, the Diligence Dimension goes even further to guide the right seller behavior.

The best Sales Processes are progressive and well defined. They include key seller activities and decision points as well as important client behaviors to observe. These client indicators are critical because they screen out salesperson subjectivity. If a client is not demonstrating the appropriate level of engagement at a given stage, then the salesperson cannot accurately grade that particular deal as being further along in the Sales Process than the client evidence indicates. This consistent method of evaluating deals is essential for you as a sales leader. The more objective your team can be about a sales opportunity, the stronger your forecasting and pipeline management activities will be.

There should also be a layer within the Sales Process that speaks to how your buyers decide to make a purchase—a view into their world. This concept is sometimes called buyer-centric selling. However, rather than considering this as a separate model or approach, its wisdom and insight should fold nicely into your internal Sales Process. This added awareness helps to further guide a salesperson's behavior during client interactions to ensure that everyone is getting what they need out of these exchanges. The better these buyer needs are met during each interaction, the stronger client indicators will be and the faster a deal will progress through the Sales Process.

When it comes time to implement a Sales Process, follow the path outlined for rolling out a Sales Methodology. Ideally, it is best to introduce these two at the same time. Identify the distinctions for your sales team so that they can see the symbiotic relationship. Again, start with providing clarity around the sales vision (what and why), followed by the Sales Methodology, which speaks to how we sell (including our sale type), and the Sales Process, which adds science and rigor to help us track our opportunities. The Diligence Dimensions are the connective tissue.

Specific to implementing the Sales Process, stay mindful of ways to integrate language into the sales function. If your Sales Methodology uses language like *learn, explore,* and *closing,* carry that language over, and use it throughout the Sales Process. In other words, don't have two different words that mean the same thing. This only confuses salespeople. Second, work Sales Process stages into your CRM, internal reports, and other tracking tools. The content of your Sales Process needs to become part of your team's routine conversations.

PREPARE FOR IMPACT

Taking these important steps as a sales leader is a catalyst for driving consistency into the sales function. When you help salespeople really internalize your sales strategy, it keeps them oriented in the right direction. For example, if they understand the value of your solution, it keeps them from knife-fighting on price.

As salespeople come to understand the type of sale they are engaged with and how they are to approach their customer interactions, then you will start seeing early indicators that your efforts around Sales Methodology are beginning to work. Then, as your Sales Process becomes the norm for how sellers pursue, grade, and report on their opportunities, things will get more accurate and quantifiable. As the Diligence Dimensions—Growing Relationships, Situational Intelligence, Securing Information, Intentional Listening, Persuasive Communication, Personal Ownership, Time Planning, Service Mindset, Winning Drive, and Inner Resolve—take root alongside your Sales Methodology and Sales Process, each working together as key pillars of your Sales Effectiveness Program, you will begin to see the unmistakable signs of consistently productive salesperson behavior.

Chapter 14

Developing Diligence

As a fast follow-on to rolling out a Sales Methodology and Sales Process comes the focus on developing skill and ability in salespeople. With this in mind, creating a comprehensive Sales Development Plan becomes the third important pillar of a strong Sales Effectiveness Program.

When creating a Sales Development Plan, it is helpful to approach development as a spectrum. Anchoring one end of that spectrum is competencies. On the other end stands capabilities. Sometimes these two terms are used interchangeably, but it is important to recognize the way that they are different.

Competencies define the skills, knowledge, abilities, and behaviors required for high performance at work or more specifically in a sales role. Capabilities are about application and mastery. In other words, capabilities are competencies in action. The distance between competencies and capabilities on the development spectrum is where you must define a tailored learning path to get your salespeople where they need to go. This path, how you will move your salespeople from competency to capability, is what gets memorialized and documented within a Sales Development Plan.

In the same way that the Diligence Dimensions thread through a Sales Methodology and Sales Process to provide added depth and horsepower, so too do they play an important role in the Sales Development Plan. Here, the Diligence Dimensions offer sales leaders both a set of baseline competencies *and* a clear path forward to build salesperson capability. The dimensions define what seller excellence looks like (competencies) and provide example behaviors and habits for salespeople to adopt and apply in order to improve their performance (capabilities).

Using the Diligence Dimensions as a baseline for drafting a Sales Development Plan is a shortcut for getting started. As a next step, the leadership team should come together to assess and prioritize current performance gaps and align learning types to address gaps/plan goals. Then they will determine who will own (and fine-tune) the Sales Development Plan and how to resource its implementation. We'll dive into more specifics around these steps in just a bit.

DON'T START WITH SALES TRAINING

Taking this plan-based approach to sales development is a significant leadership differentiator. There comes a point in time at every growth company when the business's senior leaders realize that they need to get serious about developing their people. They will often start by coming together around the planning table and debating whether it makes sense to insource development efforts, outsource them, or perhaps even do a little of both. It is *very* common for these discussions to get tactical quickly. Even the most strategic business leaders will suggest that the team get started with some kind of sales training right out of the gate. This is because to many leaders, the idea of putting a sales team through a training class seems very tangible. It appears to be a logical place to start. When this happens, the planning conversations go from wondering how to develop their salespeople to whether the team thinks it makes sense to insource or outsource a sales training solution. These are obviously very different discussions and outcomes.

After the leadership team starts down the road of tactical training, usually someone is tasked with exploring available options. They begin an internet search and maybe talk with a few people in their network, only to soon realize that this effort has produced a mind-numbing number of possibilities. Whether this research is focused on informing the decision to insource training or on creating a list of potential vendors, it is easy to become overwhelmed by the sheer volume of information.

When this happens, leaders often respond in a predictably conservative way, thinking they should start off on a smaller, more controlled scale. Because there are so many options, there's this collective reflex around hedging. To avoid putting all eggs (time, money) in one basket, perhaps it makes sense to invest in a single sales training webinar or pilot workshop and see how it goes. Of course, while the initial leadership decision may be to stay small at first, both in scope and in investment, invariably things start to get complicated.

Usually the rubber meets the road when people start talking about implementation. Whether these are vendor-led conversations or internal dialogue, it's through these discussions that leaders realize pretty quickly that running a workshop or buying some online learning isn't the same thing as developing salespeople. Consider the following list of important questions:

- Do we have a set of objective competencies or performance criteria to which we are developing our salespeople?
- How do we know what kind of training our people actually need?
- What would starting small look like for us?

- How will we assess group needs versus individual needs?
- Who on our team has the expertise to know whether a behavior or performance gap is best addressed through training, coaching, or other forms of development?
- Where do we get validated content that represents real best practice?
- If we invest time and energy into creating homegrown content, how can we evaluate its strength and relevance? What is the cost of providing our people with mediocre content?
- What is the right mix of blended learning?
- What are the right learning outcomes?
- Who on our team has the skills to facilitate learning, not just talk at people?
- How will we implement adult learning principles and create a strong pre-/post training strategy?
- Who can manage implementation, track success, and continue to identify gaps?
- How can we leverage our managers in this process?
- How will we gather, analyze, and apply training feedback?
- How can we continue evaluating behavior gaps and prescribing the right fix?

The painful reality is that most companies are reactive in addressing these issues. They get off on the wrong foot with development from day one, spending years and countless resources trying to dig themselves out of layer upon layer of tactical training decisions. But this isn't evident at first. Quite the opposite, actually. Most leaders feel good because they've spent $50,000 on a vendor's workshop and perhaps some online learning. However, the simple truth is that when the previously listed questions go unaddressed, there is virtually no way that a single training event or even a small series of events can be successful by itself. They may produce a quick spike in knowledge, but without an enduring anchor or plan for post training reinforcement, that knowledge will fade with time. This is why it's not a great idea to start with just sales training. Without a development strategy to drive the right investment for leaders and create traction with salespeople, most episodic training knowledge will be lost in a matter of weeks.

Of course, the flip side is that if your business addresses these questions with a more holistic Sales Development Plan, then your chances for success increase exponentially. It is critical to build the first phase of a Sales Development Plan that covers as many of these bases as possible and yet remains flexible enough to expand and evolve as the company grows. A well-constructed Sales Development Plan will not only address each of the previously mentioned considerations but also will guide leaders on any internal headcount you might need to operationalize the plan. It will also reveal specific opportunities where you may want to bring on new team members or engage solution providers. Otherwise, it is very common to unintentionally hire the wrong people and spend a good deal of money on vendor solutions that are essentially just a flash in the pan.

BUILDING THE PLAN

Building a Sales Development Plan may not be the easiest initiative at first. However, the payoff is exceptional clarity around how to get started and keep going in the hard work of developing salespeople. The insights derived from the planning process will help leaders navigate the complex waters of training methods, content selection, adult learning principles, and effective implementations. Becoming more informed in each of these areas will ensure that the business is investing wisely, at the right level, and in the right strategy based on where the company is today.

The planning process should begin with senior leadership, primarily because it is important to understand where the business is at today and where it's going, and to have an honest discussion about performance gaps. This is also critical for top-down buy-in around strategy and budget. These planning conversations should start with the leadership team debating this critical question: *How capable are our salespeople today, and where do we need them to be?*

That last part—where we need them to be—implies both the level at which you need your salespeople operating today and where you expect they will need to be over the next three to five years. In other words, planning discussions must factor in what skills and abilities salespeople need to have in order to achieve current revenues and what will be required to thrive at the next level of expected company growth and in a marketplace with even greater complexities.

One example of a current ability might be building sales team skills around persuasively communicating the value of your solutions in a client-focused way. Perhaps this is an important step up the capability ladder from what the team is doing today: selling on price. An example of future capabilities might be persuasively using data to build a business case for customers on why your solution is the best option. While selling on value may be a critical must-have for where the business is today, using data as another layer of persuasion may be equally critical in the future as buyers get more savvy and have additional choices to consider. It is easy to see a development path taking shape: selling on price → selling on value → selling with data.

Once leadership has detailed a list of performance gaps between where sellers are today and where they need to be, this information will factor into goal setting for the Sales Development Plan. Identifying the right goals is critical for bringing clarity around developmental priorities. The best goal setting is informed by the following:

1. Building an objective inventory of skill gaps
2. Obtaining manager context and added performance insights
3. Gaining salesperson ideas and input

This balanced approach to creating goals will ensure that the plan isn't too dependent on one group's bias or opinions. When the information gleaned from each of these sources is cataloged into a Venn diagram of sorts, the areas of agreement or overlap will help form the initial goals of a Sales Development Plan. An example set of shared goals that guides the direction and priorities of a plan may be to do the following:

1. Enable our sales team to advance and track opportunities using the shared language and stages of our company's Sales Process.
2. Teach salespeople how to sell persuasively in competitive scenarios.
3. Educate salespeople on our company's tool kit and resources to support persuasive selling.
4. Ensure that sellers understand how our business makes money and how to structure the most profitable deals.

With a set of goals established, the next component of a Sales Development Plan is to link those goals to learning. In other words, each goal should be addressed through the right type of learning to bring about behavior change. There is a right and a wrong answer here. Some developmental priorities cannot be adequately addressed through some types of learning. Generally speaking, there are four types of learning: Live, Self-Paced, Coaching, and Tools and Resources. Each one of these learning types has its own inherent strengths and limitations. This is why it's important as part of the Sales Development planning process to assign the most effective learning type to each of your development goals to ensure maximum effectiveness. Using Tools and Resources to reinforce Live, Self-Paced, and Coaching will create staying power and behavior consistency over time. In the simplest of terms, learning reinforcement is about a plan to refresh key training or coaching concepts and stimulate learner application of those concepts in their work.

Let's break down these four types into greater detail:

- *Type 1: Live Learning* is about bringing people together in person, either in a classroom or virtually. Since this same-time-same-place learning is one of the most effective training methods (and the highest cost), it is important to invest wisely. Live Learning should be tapped to address only the highest-priority sales development goals where real-time, interactive training is critical. It's best to bring people together for Live Learning on a quarterly basis if you can afford it or at least twice a year.
- *Type 2: Self-Paced Learning* is individual learning that a seller participates in on their own time. As an example, salespeople may be provided with access to e-learning or computer-based courses, games, and other on-demand platform-based classes. One of the most common mistakes companies make with this sort of learning is buying these resources in bulk and rolling them out indiscriminately, usually on an LMS. In order for this do-it-yourself learning to be effective, it needs to be carefully curated and connected back to a salesperson's work so that they can make sense of it. There also has to be some quality control

to ensure that any off-the-shelf-type learning aligns to the way salespeople need to sell at *your* company. It is important that you do not leave it up to the salesperson to try to figure out how some generic on-demand class ties back to their company's Sales Methodology and Process.

- *Type 3: Coaching* is one of the most effective forms of both learning and reinforcement, but it can also be the most time-consuming. Typically, managers are tasked with coaching salespeople, but at times companies may also hire the services of a professional coach. Coaching can be impactful for two reasons. First, it offers personal attention. Second, it's contextually relevant because the most common coaching topics are centered on a seller's current opportunities. Of course, not all coaching is good coaching. If managers are calling it coaching but are really directing or talking at a salesperson, then they should expect minimal impact on long-term development and behavior change. Similarly, if managers are leaning too much into opinion-based coaching rather than content or process-based coaching, then this is also far less effective—sellers in this case aren't learning best practices, just what their manager wants them to do. The best coaching involves strong manager skills, good content, and relevant context.
- *Type 4: Tools and Resources* are critical to help drive learning and coaching efforts into the salesperson's everyday work. These could be checklists, cheat sheets, quick refresher videos, specialized platforms or software, templates, playbooks, or anything else that helps sellers do their work faster, with greater consistency. Tools and Resources come alongside Live Learning, Self-Paced Learning, and Coaching to reinforce key concepts and help salespeople apply what they learned to actual sales opportunities. They should always be

rolled out in conjunction with the other learning types. As an example, after a class on Navigating Client Objections, participants might be given a cheat sheet referencing the "Top Common Objections and Responses." While Live Learning, Self-Paced Learning, or Coaching efforts represent the what and the why when it comes to a salesperson's learning, Tools and Resources most often further the how. Each Tool and Resource should always be connected to your Sales Methodology and Sales Process.

Based on the practice of assigning learning types to development goals and factoring in a layer of reinforcement, here is how a Sales Development Plan might start to take shape based on two of the prior example goals:

Agreed-Upon Team Development Goals	**Assigning Learning Types**
Enable our sales team to advance and track opportunities using the shared language and stages of our company's Sales Process.	**Initial Learning** *Type 1—Live Learning:* Assemble sales team to learn Sales Process stages and new shared language. *Type 4—Tools and Resources:* Provide one-page cheat sheet of Sales Process and embed into CRM accordingly. **Added Learning/Reinforcement** *Type 3—Coaching:* Each manager will have the Sales Process out and visible during coaching conversations and will weave process language into opportunity discussions.

Teach salespeople how to sell persuasively in competitive scenarios.	**Initial Learning** *Type 2—Self-Paced Learning:* Sellers will be assigned a three-part on-demand learning series that teaches a three-step process to sell against the competition; the invitation to join this learning will be customized with Sales Methodology and Process context to ensure relevancy. *Type 1—Live Learning:* Assemble sales team to role-play/group practice what they learned via on-demand; team will practice with real-life client scenarios and receive instructor feedback. **Added Learning/Reinforcement** *Type 4—Tools and Resources:* Provide a playbook of sample scripts on how sellers should sell against your competition.

This early draft example plan might easily cover one quarter's worth of training resources (money and time) for most growth companies—for others it may represent two quarters' worth. Regardless, it is best to go through this exercise for each of the shared goals and then prioritize which goals to tackle in which order. Ideally, a Sales Development Plan would cover two years of goals and proposed learning so that various initiatives are spread out.

When companies try to cram too much learning into a compressed window, it overwhelms salespeople and stresses out the internal team. Instead of going to the appropriate depth and getting results around a specific goal, trying to deploy too much learning becomes akin to eating dinner at a buffet—you may put a little of everything on your plate to try, but you probably will fill up quickly and not feel as nourished as if you had eaten a well-planned, three-course meal. The same is true for salespeople learning. Trying to do too much in a short time only serves to give sellers a little of everything but not a whole lot of anything. Prioritizing goals and spreading out a Sales Development Plan across a few years ensures that each phase of training, coaching, and reinforcement has the time required to confirm that new concepts are applied and the best salesperson behaviors take root. Appropriate spacing also helps to level load implementation responsibilities, which can otherwise lead to internal overwhelm.

Once you have established goals and priorities and have assigned learning types, the remaining two components of building a Sales Development Plan include implementation and resourcing. At the earliest stages of formalizing a development strategy, chances are many growth companies won't have a well-staffed internal sales training team. The focus on sales training is an important differentiator from other types of training such as technology (hard skills) or other HR (soft skills) training initiatives. Sales development or training efforts are focused toward driving measurable performance results. There is both a defined art and a science to building and fine-tuning salesperson capability so that it impacts revenue. Contrast this against nonrevenue-generating employee development like safety or workplace harassment—both important, just in a different category.

When it comes time to make a specific, next-level investment in developing salesperson capability, there are two important considerations: Who will be responsible for leading this endeavor, and where will we source content? These two decision points are critical to effectively operationalizing a Sales Development Plan.

STAFFING A TRAINING TEAM

Chances are when you're ready to implement the Sales Development Plan, it will require a personnel investment. This decision will involve either repositioning existing team members with the right experience and skill potential or hiring new people. In either case, determining the right coverage model requires understanding the different types of learning and development professionals, what they do, and where they fit within the plan. There are generally four types of professionals to consider—those who

- lead a sales training team;
- write, shape, and package sales training content;
- specialize in facilitation, training, or teaching people; and
- manage implementation-related projects and administer learning tech.

In talking with potential candidates, it is very likely that some will have experience in each of these areas. However, the key is to dig for their true specialization and expertise. Each of those roles is quite different from one another and requires different skill sets. True, all-in-one candidates are extraordinarily rare—most people have activities that they are more passionate about and thus have devoted more time toward cultivating. Growth companies need the right people in the right roles to implement their Sales Development Plan. Hiring someone who appears to be a jack-of-all-trades might seem like a money-saver on paper, but the downside of being a master of none is mediocre implementation.

Now for the right coverage model. Implementing a two-year Sales Development Plan requires, at a minimum, someone to serve as the internal owner and manager of the plan. While leadership may define and prioritize the goals, it is this internal owner who will perfect and implement the plan itself. So, for most smaller to medium growth companies looking to make a first hire, it's best to seek a hands-on senior sales training manager with about five to seven years of experience who can do this work.

Next, it is important to source validated sales content that will plug into the various parts of the Sales Development Plan. For example, if a Sales Development Plan has a year-one priority that calls for rolling out a foundational sales training, then this content must either be created internally by a skilled sales training designer or you might go shopping for it. Whether we are talking about content being used within Live Learning, Self-Paced Learning, or material to support Coaching, obtaining strong sales content is essential. Training without best practice content just boils down to idea- or opinion-swapping.

Finally, you need to establish who teaches the content to your people. In other words, who is at the front of the room or on the screen delivering Live Learning? Typically, this is an experienced facilitator/trainer who is energetic and steeped in the business of selling. Some have even carried the bag themselves and developed many different ways to engage groups of salespeople.

Sales managers are *not* the best people for this role. So many growth companies think that they can do a train-the-trainer workshop for their managers and that it will turn them into trainers. This rarely works. It is far better to leverage your sales managers in a real-deal coaching capacity than to expect that they put on what is often a very ill-fitting training hat. Managers already have a full-time job managing, and most will resist efforts to assume a training role due to lack of bandwidth, comfort level issues, or both. Even if they nod in agreement that they will undertake this new layer to their job, the reality is that they won't do it well, if at all. So sales leaders must calculate the business cost of this approach if the odds are against its success from the very beginning.

For these reasons, early personnel investments might be the following:

- Senior sales training manager—the quarterback who owns/perfects the Sales Development Plan and manages internal implementation
- Sales training designer or an external sales content source—the validated/best practice sales training content that plugs into the Sales Development Plan, representing what gets trained in Live Learning, Self-Paced Learning, and even Coaching support
- Sales facilitator/trainer—represents who trains Live Learning at your company and may serve as added Coaching support for sales managers

Some companies that want to maximize their budget and roster of full-time employees may opt to hire a full-time senior sales training manager while identifying and budgeting for a part-time or contract sales training designer and facilitator to start.

EXTERNALLY SOURCING CONTENT

Having a personnel formula to jump-start the implementation of a Sales Development Program is the first important step. Once you have identified someone who will own and manage the plan, next up is taking a deeper dive into options for sourcing sales content. For the moment, we'll take a look at things to consider when outsourcing content from an external provider, and then we'll talk through the reality of homegrown, in-house solutions.

When engaging with various external content providers, keep in mind that sales is their business. This means that most are well practiced and able to quickly articulate many of the common performance challenges that a growing company is facing. Chances are high that you'll recognize many of them in your own organization, and this will increase your confidence in the content provider. As these conversations unfold, providers will suggest a content and possibly a services package that they believe is the right fix and formula for your sales team. If they are persuasive, their recommendations are going to seem tailor-made for your business. However, keep in mind that this solution is most likely the same content and services they supply to hundreds, if not thousands, of other clients. It's an advantage to know this going into these conversations so that you can dig deeper on the details and ensure that there is a genuinely strong fit between a content provider's solution and your business. Use your Sales Development Plan as a way to probe. Ask the provider to offer specifics on how their content directly connects to each of the performance gaps covered in your plan. If you want them to go the extra mile before you invest, ask that they map their content to your Sales Development Plan and then ask for a content walk-through so that you can compare it with the map they've created and see the fit for yourself. Taking these extra steps while you're evaluating solutions is a much better alternative than pulling the trigger after a cursory review, only to go to all the trouble of rolling out a one-size-fits-all content set ill-suited to your sales team. Continue digging to understand services like customization or creation to better comprehend the benefits and limitations. Many companies think they are getting customized content only to realize after the deal that a content provider will do only superficial customization.

Speaking of other realizations that come after signing a

content provider deal, companies that are just getting their feet wet with outsourcing are often surprised by how little service they get from the provider compared to how much support they *actually* need. While providers may express appreciation for where your business is in its evolution, ultimately they aren't going to assume responsibility for how your Sales Development Plan is implemented—they are there to ensure that you get your content. Generally, that's it. Recognizing that these external providers work hard to stay in their lane is important. You want to get into these relationships with clear expectations around the many things that your internal team will be responsible for when plugging externally sourced content into the Sales Development Plan. Understanding the limited but important role that content plays in the overall responsibility of implementing the Sales Development Plan will ensure that balls don't drop and that the plan produces the best developmental results.

As a quick analogy, imagine that you and some friends have tickets to see your favorite comedian or band. It is up to you to get to the show on time. You have to secure a babysitter. Figure out who is going to drive or where you will meet up. Deal with traffic, parking, the long lines of people waiting to get inside. Then you have to find your seat and possibly slow-walk your way to the restroom. More lines. Perhaps you and your friends start looking up bars or restaurants to hit up after the show. Then boom, the lights go down, the announcer comes on, and within minutes the performance begins. After two hours or so, it's back to the drudgery of baby-stepping your way through the massive crowds out to the street and then figuring out what's next with your friends. We all love to watch a live performance, but it takes planning, preparation, cooperation, and action before and after the show to actually get a return on your entertainment investment.

Contrast this reality with that of the entertainer. That individual is well paid and in many cases a bit pampered as they prepare to take the stage for a few hours and do what they do best—perform. They aren't concerned with how their audience gets there or back home. The entertainer is there to do their best and leave the rest to others.

In this scenario, of course, the entertainer is the sales training or content provider. While most are prepared to do their best for clients, they stay laser focused on their specialty—after all, they are in business too, and getting in and out is how they make their money. For example, you may get an external provider who focuses on in-person, instructor-led training—what we've been referring to as Live Learning. In this case, a client would typically pay one fee to license the content (usually contained within a workbook) and another fee that covers their certified trainer to deliver a predetermined number of classroom sessions. Any travel expenses are always extra. If the goal is to have these providers certify your trainer, the fee structure is similar, but it is usually higher because they are effectively handing their content and methods over to your team, and they need to obtain greater licensing revenue, sort of like a buyout. In another scenario, you might have a provider who offers a bulk catalog of e-learning, either by itself to use on your existing platform or together with a platform license. In this case, the provider's lane is to supply bulk content to serve as Self-Paced Learning options for your salespeople. That's it.

All the other factors and complexities involved with implementing a Sales Development Plan to ensure that these learning efforts actually take hold and create behavior change isn't something that most of these providers will take on—their business models don't support that sort of service continuation. Recognizing this distinction is important for a few reasons.

Sometimes companies that are just starting to level up their development efforts will think about outsourcing most of the components of their Sales Development Plan (content, trainers, coaches, tools, tech). Usually speed is the motivator here. However, this approach means managing several different provider relationships—each with their own method, language, fees, and service limitations. This patchwork approach can strain your internal teams and often feels disjointed to the sales team.

The better alternative is to keep your Sales Methodology, Sales Process, and Sales Development Plan at the center of conversations with content providers. Require potential providers to show you how their content will seamlessly plug into your Sales Development Plan and drive priorities for year one and year two. That way, you'll be able to create a short list of those who have a deep enough catalog to grow with you over a few years and maintain some measure of continuity for salespeople. As multiple proposals come in featuring content intended to drive your Sales Development Plan, it will also make it a lot easier to do apples-to-apples comparisons around price and value.

CREATING HOMEGROWN CONTENT

While sourcing sales content through vendors is very popular, many companies opt to develop their own content internally. Or perhaps the strategy is more of a hybrid. For example, maybe Self-Paced Learning is sourced through a vendor while Live Learning, Coaching Support, and Tools and Resources are created internally.

Doing this work well and at the speed of business requires the skills of an experienced sales training instructional designer. If you can find someone who is both a subject matter expert (SME) in sales and who knows how to design adult learning, this is ideal. That's because when someone is just an instructional designer, they have to be paired with an SME. If you are relying on your internal leaders or managers to serve as an SME, it could take dozens of hours of their time being interviewed by an instructional designer every step of the way as they work to develop content. An instructional designer with sales expertise will be able to connect the dots and fill in the gaps.

Of course, all this assumes that you have enough subject matter knowledge in-house to begin with. To avoid building in-house training off good ideas and opinions, consider investing in access to sales research that the designer can use (with permission and/or attribution) to influence the training materials that are created. Combining your Sales Methodology, Sales Process, research best practice, and other insights from your internal leaders should be enough for a good designer to synthesize the material and create solid training content. Other resources that may be required for investment planning include a design software package, graphics, proofreading support, stock photography, and other related tools for branding requirements.

The major consideration related to creating sales content internally is time. Even if you have the right in-house expertise and a strong instructional designer, so much else also goes into content creation. For example, a sixty-minute virtual Live Learning class would essentially cover one sales topic, like handling objections. Just sixty minutes of virtual content would likely take a good instructional designer about three to four weeks to create. This includes the following:

- Planning learning objectives
- Interviewing SMEs for best practices on objection handling
- Writing a course outline (what gets covered, when, and for how long)

- Designing and developing a prework strategy for learners
- Authoring teachable skills content (objection handling)
- Designing and developing worksheets for learners
- Designing and developing slides or other visuals
- Layering in adult learning strategy to ensure engagement
- Conducting a walk-through with sales leadership, gathering and implementing feedback
- Writing trainer/facilitator notes (content, timing, and how best to use the tech)
- Conducting a walk-through with trainer/facilitator

With this general scope of work in mind for a single unit of content (objection handling), it becomes clear how the scope and required time exponentially increase as requests for more content come in. A single instructional designer creating in-house content might take six to eight months to develop a full two-day workshop on selling skills. If they're juggling multiple priorities at once, the timetable lengthens accordingly. Things like designing training in software or on a platform is another layer that adds more time.

It is important to recognize what is involved when creating homegrown content because it underscores how capable your internal sales training instructional designer needs to be and how time-intensive this work actually is.

IMPLEMENTATION STRATEGY

After you've finalized the priority goals, learning types, supporting staff, and content sourcing details with a Sales Development Plan, the focus then turns toward implementation strategy. In this case, the business owner of this plan, likely your new sales training manager, is responsible for how best to sequence, arrange, and deploy plan resources in a way that moves sellers from where they are on the competency-to-capability spectrum to where they need to go in order to drive revenue goals.

A strong Sales Development Plan implementation strategy addresses the following:

- Offers a way to measure the current levels of salesperson competency to establish a baseline for development
- Analyzes this data to identify group and individual trends to further prioritize when to roll out the various learning contained within the plan
- Maps approved sales training content to each component of the Sales Development Plan to ensure relevance and linkage
- Establishes review protocols for all sales training content to ensure connection back to Sales Methodology, Sales Process, and competencies
- Maintains high standards for content to support adult learning (shorter length, substantive, practical)
- Creates an internal manager coaching program to ensure that these people leaders have the skills and resources to coach consistently
- Monitors and manages reinforcement efforts to ensure the stickiness of Live and Self-Paced Learning investments
- Designs an internal feedback channel and system to collect, analyze, and apply feedback to support continuous improvement
- Remeasures salesperson competencies at planned intervals to gauge improvement and any emerging gaps
- Tracks and reports program highlights and insights to company leadership

The role of measurement as part of implementation cannot

be overstated. Most business leaders are eager to get their hands on some sort of objective learning metrics. They want to know the return on investment (ROI) of their outlay in training. Unfortunately, this is often much harder to assess than it sounds. One of the reasons it's so difficult is because many companies don't go through the organic process of building their Sales Development Plan. Without the rigor of drawing a straight line from business priorities to developmental gaps to measuring current competencies (baseline) to learning and coaching to remeasuring competencies and evaluating key performance initiatives (KPIs), it is impossible to gain ROI insights.

The other reason why the ROI on learning investments is elusive for many companies is because there is too much inconsistency within the sales function. If sales leadership hasn't integrated Sales Methodology and Process or competencies into the work stream, then there is too much variability in play. Salespeople are doing their own variation of what you want them to do and using their preferred jargon to describe it. Variability is the enemy of consistency, and you need consistency to measure results.

Despite these challenges, sales leaders don't have to settle for no measurement at all or the very limited insights that come from systems reporting, which don't account for the impact of Live Learning, some offline forms of Self-Paced Learning, or Coaching inputs. The easiest way to get started with some data is to look to competencies—in other words, the Diligence Dimensions. By taking a baseline measurement of where sellers are before you start investing in sales development efforts and then tracking that baseline, it will be easy to see how all the learning types, content, and people resources are working together to produce better outcomes.

MANAGER COACHING

Finally, manager coaching continues to be the great enabler of any Sales Development Plan. The ability to get managers coaching consistently over time will make or break an implementation strategy. While tasking managers with facilitating a sales training workshop is typically a bridge too far, they should be expected and incentivized around the quality and frequency of their coaching efforts.

In many growth companies, there is a disconnect between more senior leaders and the management team that supervises individual salespeople. Company leaders will passionately extol the virtues of coaching and suggest that it's something their managers do regularly. The hard truth is that most of them don't.

There are two common reasons why managers don't coach—time and knowledge. When coaching becomes part of their bonus compensation, that tends to eliminate the time objection. However, many well-meaning managers *do* want to coach, but they genuinely don't know how. When this happens, they revert to telling salespeople how they would handle a particular situation. While this may end up being good advice, it is not developmental. However, if you were to ask these managers if they coach their people, most, if not all, would say yes, they do. These well-meaning managers miss the point that giving advice or telling a salesperson what to do is not building their capability. The first step in changing this dynamic is to build awareness and help managers recognize the difference between managing and coaching. This is one of the first important steps in cultivating managers to become an essential lever in implementing a Sales Development Plan. A strong support plan for managers requires context, capability, content, and continuity.

Managers must be taught that when they put their coaching hat on, they are moving into a new mode. Instead of inspecting and directing, they are engaging and teaching. To do this well, they need to be experts in recognizing the connection between their company's Sales Methodology and Sales Process as well as its sales competencies. Once they are conversationally intelligent about how we sell (Sales Methodology), how to track our opportunities (Sales Process), and how we build capability in our people (Competencies), then they are able to pull this common language and stated expectations into their coaching conversations. Now real-life client opportunities provide important context for showing salespeople how to apply knowledge and skills. Only your managers are in this unique position to help salespeople get better on the job as they work with clients.

Working with the context of real-life opportunities, managers can extract their lessons by tapping into the relevant competencies. For example, Situational Intelligence and Persuasive Communication may be excellent coaching topics for an opportunity where the seller is about to make a presentation to a diverse group. To ensure that the coaching conversation is substantial, the manager can pull content points from competencies like Situational Intelligence and Persuasive Communication and either indicate specific, helpful nuggets during the coaching conversation itself or assign it as homework for the salesperson to review before their client meeting.

Finally, the only way to get traction is to maintain coaching continuity. In other words, treat these developmental conversations as a chain of events. The salesperson should know that they will be accountable to apply information discussed in the coaching conversation and that there will be a follow up. For this reason, it is important for managers to establish coaching routines with their people. While it is good to have episodic, unplanned coaching, at least half of all coaching discussions should be scheduled in advance. This way both the manager and the salesperson can be proactive about skill development and not always reactive.

When managers across the sales function can establish a continuous habit around coaching, it not only will help salespeople get better results on actual client deals but also will help to consistently advance Sales Development Plan implementation.

Chapter 15

Selecting Diligence

When a Sales Methodology, Sales Process, and Sales Development Plan are in place, each of these components will be working together in harmony to create a foundation for consistency. The more that leaders, managers, and salespeople are using common language and adopting performance expectations, the more traction and momentum will materialize.

As the business continues to grow, so too will there be new opportunities for salespeople to level up their skills and capability. So every few years the Sales Development Plan priorities and goals will need to evolve so that salesperson capability can keep pace with new demands. Given the dedication and resources required to sustain this development effort across your existing sales team, it is important to take a fresh look at how you bring in new sales talent. As you begin seeing some payoff from implementing the Sales Development Plan, chances are you want to import new people who are wired for quick success within your organization.

This likely means some smart adjustments to existing selection practices. There are a few ways to pull through some of the components of your Sales Development Plan so that they influence how prospective candidates are screened, evaluated, and ultimately hired. Once again, the Diligence Framework offers an advantage. The same ten dimensions that define sales excellence for your existing sales team can support efforts to identify and hire new team members. Leveraging these dimensions throughout the selection process will bring continuity and help the hiring team objectively identify only the best candidates.

THE CASE FOR CONSISTENCY

In most growing companies, the people who are responsible for bringing new talent into their organization are often wearing a lot of hats. Competing priorities and aggressive deadlines can get in the way of doing what feels like the nice-to-have work of improving the process and practice of hiring new people. When running from one meeting to another and dealing with an overflowing in-box, it can be difficult to take a step back from the daily mire to evaluate ways to adjust or fine-tune the hiring process, even if doing so promises to improve the quality of new hires brought into the business.

Of course, there are real costs associated with getting the hiring equation wrong. If a promising new hire winds up flaming out, it isn't too difficult to calculate some of those costs. When that new hire is a quota-carrying salesperson who's falling well short of revenue expectations nine to ten months in, then those costs can compound quickly for the business. You not only have the traditional hiring costs associated with candidate acquisition and the time of various team members interviewing that person but also when the new underperformer is a salesperson, you must add in the costs of lost revenue productivity. There's also the potential of lackluster client experience and other intangibles.

For these reasons, it is important to make strides in perfecting how we hire sales talent. Increasing consistency around how your company short-lists, interviews, and selects new salespeople will improve the likelihood of bringing in those who are a cultural fit and who have the qualities necessary to succeed in *your* sales system.

SELECTION WATCHOUTS

1. The majority of candidate information is subjective.
2. The job description is wrong.
3. Just because a salesperson did well in their last organization doesn't mean they will replicate that success in yours.
4. The hiring team (HR and sales) operates in silos.

Evolving your processes and practices requires an honest analysis of what is working and what isn't. During this assessment, chances are you will uncover some watchouts. These little bad habits and hinderances can creep in slowly over time when people are running a mile a minute. They can also be a by-product of the disconnect that happens when departments like the sales team choose to be the hiring manager while looking to their colleagues in HR to shepherd the hiring process itself. While this sharing of duties happens for a number of reasons, any disconnect between departments can contribute to hit-or-miss hires.

Recognizing the presence of these watchouts in your organization can help you quickly identify important changes before undertaking the next hiring blitz. While we are primarily talking about improving how salespeople are hired, in reality the following recommendations can apply to hiring candidates for nonsales roles as well.

With this in mind, one of the first watchouts occurs when *the majority of candidate information is subjective.* Even if an organization uses a set of competencies to define sales excellence with their existing team, if they aren't pulled through the interview process, then candidates will end up being evaluated more subjectively than objectively. Even when techniques like behavioral-based interviewing are employed, without a rigorous scoring system to grade answers, the interviewer's opinion around how well the candidate answered the question is what will prevail. When hiring decisions are primarily made based on how the candidate subjectively positions their past experience on top of how company interviewers subjectively feel about the candidate's personality and the answers they gave to questions, then it's impossible to know for sure how well that candidate will objectively perform posthire.

Another watchout stemming from not integrating competencies into the hiring process is quite often that *the job description is wrong*. Sometimes companies will use a job description that is a few years old, meaning that it hasn't been updated to coincide with the ways that the role may have evolved. Other times, it could just be flat-out inaccurate. As an example, a job description may read like it's hiring for strictly a farmer-type or account-based selling role, when in actuality the company needs its salespeople to involve themselves in later stages of lead qualification before there's a bona fide opportunity. In this case, this erroneous job description will likely attract candidates who perform well at the later stages of the Sales Process (like presentations and closing) but not early on (qualifying a lead, gaining interest). Chances are when these individuals are hired, they will lack what it takes to deal with the ambiguity of a prospect who is "just looking" but not ready to buy.

If you don't alter the job description, and a candidate comes in who is charismatic and likable as all get-out, and they answer questions really well, they will probably get hired. It may take a few months to notice that they are struggling with productivity and grabbing for lower-hanging fruit deals but failing to cultivate anything new.

Just because a salesperson did well in their last organization doesn't mean they will replicate that success in yours. This watchout describes a common assumption about candidates who are attractive on paper. Just because someone's last role was with a growing SaaS company and your company is a growing SaaS company does not mean that person is going to excel in your world. Similarly, just because a candidate is well versed and connected in the financial services space and this is a vertical that your company wants to pursue does not mean that this person is the one to get you to the promised land.

The watchout is in play when interviewers don't dig for a true, factual comparison between a candidate's prior experiences and the actual environment at their company. For example, some candidates who claim to be prior top performers may in fact need a great deal of team support. In their past role, they may have had a horde of people on whom they could offload client research, collateral or case study development, demos, solution development, proposal work, and more. This candidate could have done well in that environment because of all the support available to level load their work. Will that structure and those resources be available to this individual going forward? If not, can they be as successful if they are required to be more hands-on or wear multiple hats at your company? This same comparison exercise could apply to topics like preferred manager style, working environment, process adherence, client complexity, length of sales cycle, and more.

The final watchout illustrates the pitfalls of an inadequate system for sharing candidate information. *The hiring team (HR and sales) operates in silos.* In many companies, the typical hiring process begins with a job requisition of sorts coming out of sales leadership and over to HR. Next, HR will draft a new description or pull a previous one and seek approval from sales.

Then HR will source and screen candidates, eliminating those who don't meet minimum criteria or who may have other obvious disqualifiers. HR will pass short-list candidates back to the sales team, serving at that point as more of an interview coordinator. They will often wait for a go/no-go from sales on a particular candidate before finalizing the necessary particulars to close out the candidacy of those who were not selected and follow internal processes for formalizing an offer to the choice candidate.

On paper, this process should flow back and forth, culminating in the hiring of someone spectacular. But it doesn't always happen that way. A big downside of handing the baton back and forth is that there is no real teaming and collaboration around these hires. Placing feedback or other notes within an applicant tracking system rarely closes this gap either. Each of these teams could go further together if more opportunities were in play to engage around the information gathered from potential candidates throughout the process. What may seem at first to be a time-consuming proposition would probably, in the long run, save time. When you have two teams largely operating from within their silos and, to the earlier point, around subjective candidate information, it becomes clearer how these gaps can contribute to less than the best hires.

HIRING WELL

Perhaps reviewing the prior watchouts has provided some clarity into a few ways that you can improve the process of bringing on new sales talent. Or at least shown you some things to keep an eye out for so that these issues don't take root as your company ramps up hiring to keep pace with growth. Each of the watchouts we explored can be reduced or eliminated by implementing a three-layer process for hiring sales talent:

- Start with competencies.
- Initiate a prehire meeting.
- Leverage strong comparative data.

When it comes to hiring talent, competencies help determine the skills, behaviors, and abilities necessary to perform well in a particular role. In a sales role, where strong performance is mission-critical to the business, the appropriate competency set serves as a guide for identifying candidates who are best wired to succeed. Consider the Diligence Framework dimensions as a set of competencies for hiring. Here you have five competencies—Growing Relationships, Situational Intelligence, Securing Information, Intentional Listening, and Persuasive Communication—that define the capabilities required for strong client interactions. There are also the five personal leadership competencies—Personal Ownership, Time Planning, Service Mindset, Winning Drive, and Inner Resolve—that complement the sales dimensions and increase individual effectiveness at work, whether in front of clients or when working with colleagues.

Simply plugging these into the hiring process—job descriptions, interview questions, scorecards, and more—helps the hiring team take a big step forward in making more informed decisions each step of the way. When these competencies become part of the hiring dialogue, then the gap between how we hire new people and how we develop existing people starts closing. Competencies and eventually capabilities become the consistent thread in both practices.

Team silos are easily mitigated by adopting the process of a prehire meeting between HR and sales. Here job descriptions are reviewed and fine-tuned. Discussions take place on which competencies should be prioritized during the search. The candidate process and experience will be reviewed to ensure agreement on approach and handoffs. Finally, both teams will talk about how best to share important information and how decisions will be made. Specific to sharing information, it is critical for each member of the hiring team to recognize the role of objective and subjective information. To the extent that hiring decisions can be made on a balance of strong comparative data and shared opinions, it will raise the likelihood of a successful outcome.

Ensuring that the hiring process nets that strong comparative data is essential. Implementing new practices or perfecting existing methods in order to consistently obtain comparative information on short-listed candidates will likely be the most significant adjustments made to a current hiring process. This effort involves implementing, collecting, and analyzing candidate data from three documented sources: assessment, activities, and answers.

ASSESSMENT

The impact of pulling sales competencies through the hiring process is only as good as your ability to measure them. As new candidates come in and pass through preliminary screening, now is the best time to collect the first round of objective data. You'll want to assess how a candidate is likely to behave and perform coming into your organization. A strong assessment result will suggest that they advance to the next step in the process, whereas a weaker read might suggest the need to allocate team resources to other candidates. As an example, if in the prehire meeting the team suggested that Growing Relationships, Situational Intelligence, and Service Mindset were especially important, only candidates who score above 70 percent in each of these areas may advance. Or perhaps if someone with a strong background came in with scores of 80 percent, 70 percent, and

60 percent, respectively, they might conditionally advance with the recommendation to explore the lower score through in-depth questioning.

There are a lot of choices for selection assessments on the market. A few of the most common types are personality, strengths-based, and cognitive tests. Personality tests will provide insight into how people are naturally inclined to behave, but they fall short of actually predicting performance on the job. There is no real correlation between personality and actual job performance. Strengths-based tests exist to help people identify which areas they naturally excel in so that they can use this insight to maximize their strengths on the job. While the readouts are often interesting, they only go so far toward identifying how people will behave when different parts of the Sales Process require different skills and abilities—some of which may not be a candidate's strength areas. Just as harping on weaknesses is widely considered counterproductive, focusing too much on strengths to the exclusion of developing other skills required to succeed in selling is overrated.

Cognitive tests may or may not be relevant for your business. These tests won't predict the art and science of sales performance, but they will provide data around traditional measures of intelligence such as reasoning and math. For businesses where that intellect is necessary for credibility with clients, cognitive tests may be a tool to consider.

Of course, the clear winner in the assessment category is measuring competency. Assessing how candidates score against your sales competency framework, before they come into the organization, gives you practical, comparative data. Its emphasis on behavior and situational judgment is the straightest path toward recognizing potential for accelerated sales performance posthire.

ACTIVITIES

Another opportunity to collect objective, comparative data arrives at about the midpoint in the interview process. Here a potential candidate would work on a relevant activity designed to help assess a few key factors. These may include comprehension and understanding of directions, writing quality, ability to organize thoughts or information, knowledge, resourcefulness, style, and approach. Typically, strong candidate performance on this activity would lead to being short-listed.

The best activities are designed collaboratively between the HR and sales teams. They include a few components: a summary scenario (client or business), directions to complete, and a scorecard. The scenario provides important details and prompts that should occur commonly in your business. It is helpful to the candidate if you err on the side of including more details rather than fewer details. Next comes a concise, step-by-step set of instructions for completing the activity. These should include things to think about and what needs to be covered in the candidate's response. For the response, the team should consider which format would be most revealing—an essay-style response, a short slide presentation, or perhaps a video. Out of courtesy for the candidate, it is best to not make the activity overly complex or time-consuming. Aim for developing something that most people can complete in an hour or less.

Creating a scorecard with weighted scoring to accompany the activity is necessary to produce comparative data. For example, a scorecard might look like this:

- Followed directions: 20 percent
- Persuasive communication: 20 percent
- Focused on value: 30 percent
- Response reflects good judgment: 20 percent
- Quality writing: 10 percent

As candidates complete the same activity, this scorecard makes it easy to compare performance apples to apples. When you add the results from this activity to how a candidate measures against competencies, some clarity begins to emerge. Of course, each of these data points will likely also identify areas to drill down further on specifics.

ANSWERS

This is where interview questions become a critical third point of comparative data. While many leaders are familiar with the concept of behavioral-based interviewing, the practice tends to fall short of its potential when it's partially deployed. Behavioral-based interview questions also need a scorecard-type system to help the interviewer more objectively score responses.

It is helpful to have a deep bank of questions and accompanying response scoring so that the interview team can cherry-pick the right questions to pose based on how candidates performed on the assessment and activity. For example, if a candidate short list has three people on it, and two scored lower on Situational Intelligence but did well across other priority competencies, you will want to select behavioral-based interview questions that probe further on Situational Intelligence—and you will want to pose those same questions to all three candidates to get comparative data.

The challenge comes when interviewers ask different question sets or don't consistently score responses. Getting the most out of the behavioral-based interview process involves analyzing all short-list candidates, determining which areas you want to explore, and doing that consistently with each of them so that the comparative data from their assessments, activities, and answers work together to help drive the most informed decisions.

ONBOARDING

Once a new hire comes on board, you have a continued opportunity to leverage the momentum generated during the interview and selection process. Chances are this collaborative, consistent approach has produced a wealth of insights that ultimately led to the decision to bring on a new person. Quite often, though, this information is not packaged up and pulled through from posthire into onboarding.

Assuming that a sales team has any formalized onboarding at all, typically it is a one-size-fits-all approach that quickly gets discarded once client demand picks up and the new salesperson has to partake in the all-too-familiar baptism by fire.

There is an alternative. With just a little focused effort, the HR and sales teams can work together and package up all the comparative data they collected during the hiring process. Next, by tapping into the new hire's manager, a tailored coaching plan can be put together along with thirty-, sixty-, and ninety-day performance expectations. That way, as the new hire is going through onboarding or early learning efforts, they can do so from the perspective of how it can help them meet those stated performance expectations. They can also bring targeted questions and situations to their manager during those designated coaching times.

One of the most effective methods to employ during onboarding is to get salespeople working on targeted assignments involving real-life client scenarios. This might include pairing a new salesperson with a colleague to create a few slides that describe the solution value. With input from the colleague and the manager, a new salesperson can learn where to find resources and how to persuasively communicate the value story. In this case, the new hire isn't completely responsible for the client-facing output but rather is working alongside their colleague on a real deal with targeted feedback from their manager.

Pulling together onboarding assignments that arise from each stage in the company's Sales Process will help salespeople learn the essentials quicker. Add to that curated Self-Paced Learning and eventually participating in group Live Learning, and you now have a new seller who is seamlessly integrated into the existing Sales Development Plan just like all their other colleagues.

Chapter 16

Maximizing Diligence

By now you may be inspired or intrigued by the possibilities around confronting inconsistency within the sales organization. At the same time, it can be overwhelming to think about all the work that needs to be done. But of course it's a better use of time than pursuing quick fixes that still aren't the answer. Instead, let's begin with the end in mind, by defining what the ideal state looks like and working backward from there.

Imagine the future version of your sales function that is operating in full alignment. As a sales leader, you have shed the patchwork quilt of ad hoc reactive solutions and are now presiding over the following reality:

- *There is a fortifying framework that has become the overarching umbrella for the sales function.* The team understands and leverages the Diligence Framework and its ten dimensions within their everyday work. Its coverage of both the basics and the fringe gaps addresses common issues that destabilize many teams.
- *The sales team understands how the company makes money.* They know the go-to-market plan and recognize the why behind territory, targets, and tracking.
- *There is a defined Sales Methodology and Sales Process in*

place, which leverages common language and concepts from the Diligence Framework to maintain alignment. The Sales Methodology and Sales Process are well socialized and utilized within the everyday work of the sales team.

- *The Diligence Dimensions serve as salesperson competencies.* Existing salespeople and prospective new hires are measured and assessed against these competencies to determine strengths and gaps in their ability.
- *Decisions around continued development or new-hire selection are rooted in assessment data.* Commitment to objectivity over personal opinion or bias are how things get done within the organization.
- *There is a Sales Development Plan that moves salespeople from current ability to deepened capability around the ten Diligence Dimensions and more.* The plan includes development goals, required content, learning methods, coaching strategies, and implementation specifics. There is an internal owner of this plan and resources allocated to ensure its effective implementation.
- *Managers are true coaches.* They recognize the difference between directing and teaching or guiding salespeople. Using coaching conversations, managers drive your Sales Effectiveness Program (Sales Method, Sales Process, and Sales Development Plan) into the work stream.
- *Ambitious salespeople with deep capability in the five personal leadership dimensions become ideal candidates for promotion.* Assessing and developing both core sales and personal leadership capabilities helps create a succession pipeline for the sales organization. It ensures that those being promoted from individual contributor to a manager of people have the ability to hit the ground running.

Squeezing every drop of potential out of Diligence as the antidote to inconsistency requires pulling it through the entire sales organization in this way. Otherwise, it becomes just one more idea du jour.

The framework, methodology, process, development plan, and other related approaches all band together to create the necessary infrastructure that's missing from so many sales organizations. Teams that operate from this place of alignment are much easier to fine-tune and prepare for increasing levels of growth.

Turning toward Diligence and becoming a more aligned sales function is, at its roots, a change management endeavor. For this reason, it will be important to marshal some change advocates who can help you do the work required so that confronting consistency and building capability is adopted across the board. While any good change initiative must originate at the top with leadership, bringing together a working cohort of open-minded and optimistic managers is always a best practice. With time and as the work progresses, consider adding influential salespeople or other individual contributors who can participate in and vouch for why this change will help everyone win as the company grows.

TIME TO DECLUTTER

One of the first things that change advocates can help with is a primer activity of sorts. Before building the new infrastructure, it is important to take inventory of the existing foundation. If you are like most sales organizations in growth mode, chances are you have tried to keep up with the pace of things by acquiring a lot of clutter. This might include quick fixes or certain things purchased from vendors. It could also include some homegrown materials or methods that either don't make sense any longer or don't fit with where you want to take the sales team next. Now there may be some things that *do* make sense to keep and improve upon, so it is important to start this process of infrastructure building and alignment by decluttering.

Spend some time reviewing the Diligence Framework with the change advocates. Talk through how it will inform the way you sell, how you track, and how you develop. With that in mind, ask them to consider whether existing relics should stay or go. Enjoy the feeling that comes with moving on from the things that aren't clearly positioning the team responding to growth demands. While it will take some more time to replace the clutter with the elements you want to bring in, at least the space is cleared for when that time comes. The team won't be taking classes that don't hit the mark or trying to work a process that is full of gaps. Use your change advocates, communicate what is being retired, and plant informative seeds around what's coming next.

TAKE INVENTORY

Once you've filled up that literal or figurative dumpster, it's time to bring the leadership team together for that honest assessment. The goal, as we began exploring earlier in this book, is to take inventory of where the priority issues are with salespeople and within the sales function.

Use a set of questions like these to jump-start that discussion:

- What are the challenges with how we sell (Sales Methodology)? What is the ideal state? Where do we need to focus?
- Where are the challenges with how we track opportunities (Sales Process)? What is the ideal state? Where do we need to focus?
- What are the obvious performance gaps on the sales

team (Sales Development Plan)? What is the ideal state? Where do we need to focus?

- Where are our managers falling short? What is the ideal state? Where do we need to focus?
- How can we show support for a more strongly aligned sales organization? How will we communicate this?
- What resources (people and budget) are we going to allocate toward implementing a Sales Effectiveness Program (Sales Methodology, Sales Process, Sales Development Plan)?
- Who will be the leadership sponsor over this work?

Once this information is inventoried, it can form the basis of a quarterly project plan that details how and when each element gets communicated and implemented into the organization. While the sequence and priorities of these implementation plans will vary by company, the substance is largely the same. With that in mind, let's look at a sample plan for an organization that may need to start from a fairly clean slate. As you review these two-year example plans, consider any adjustments in substance or prioritization that you might make given the actual state of your business.

Year 1: Establish Sales Effectiveness Infrastructure

	Quarter 1	Quarter 2	Quarter 3	Quarter 4
Goal	Socialize illustrative Sales Vision and new or increased focus on Sales Effectiveness.	Establish or update Sales Process and Methodology.	Create a first phase of the Sales Development Plan (SDP).	Reinforce Sales Methodology and Sales Process; begin deployment of SDP.
Key Actions	• Engage CEO or senior leadership in messaging. • Prepare highlights of Sales Effectiveness Plan. • Bring the sales team together to hear messaging.	• Determine the current sale type(s) for the company. • Develop or procure a Sales Methodology and Sales Process (weave in ten Dimensions). • Engage managers to obtain feedback at key intervals. • Code these elements into CRM or other platforms.	• Assess the sales team to determine a baseline around key capabilities (ten Dimensions). • Build initial plan around dimensions-as-competencies, priority goals, required content, learning methods, coaching strategies, and implementation specifics. • Identify a plan owner and allocate budget for people resources and content.	• Review and analyze how well the sales team has adopted the Sales Methodology and Process within their work. • Bring the sales team together to review group trends in assessment data that will show capability strengths and opportunities.

Communicate	• CEO/senior leadership shares the story of our business. • Sales leadership communicates the why behind the new focus on Sales Effectiveness, what it is, and what it means; include preview of the ten Diligence Dimensions.	• Managers to deliver Sales Methodology and Sales Process to teams via team meetings or a series of lunch and learns.	• Sales leadership and SDP owner to communicate with sales managers around key details, timing, and their role as coaches.	• Sales leadership to continue modeling and championing use of Sales Methodology and Sales Process within the work stream. • Sales managers to communicate how assessment data can help salespeople create personalized learning plans for the following year.

Year 2: Forge Alignment and Build Salesperson Capability

	Quarter 1	Quarter 2	Quarter 3	Quarter 4
Goal	Kickoff well by reinforcing the Sales Vision, Sales Methodology, and Sales Process.	Continued SDP deployment; reform new hire selection methods.	Continued SDP deployment; create phase two of SDP.	Continued SDP deployment; establish internal pipeline of candidates for promotion.
Key Actions	• Plan a kickoff meeting centered around each element of the Sales Effectiveness Program. • Tap into salespeople who are early and consistent adopters to share examples and stories. • Identify ways to recognize people who demonstrate Diligence Dimensions in their work. • Hold one priority Live Learning session.	• Hold one priority Live Learning session. • Provide a curated suite of Self-Paced Learning for the quarter. • Develop and distribute one to two Tools or Resources that support the Sales Methodology, the Sales Process, or capability/skill building. • Begin work around improving selection methods by assessing candidates against the ten Dimensions and creating uniformity around behavior-based interviewing, candidate scoring, and decision-making.	• Hold one priority Live Learning session; provide a curated suite of Self-Paced Learning for the quarter; develop and distribute one to two Tools or Resources that support the Sales Methodology, the Sales Process, or capability/skill building. • Assess salespeople again and compare current data against the baseline. Based on any continued trends, extend the SDP out to cover next year's learning. • Socialize and gain buy-in from leaders and managers.	• Hold one priority Live Learning session; provide a curated suite of Self-Paced Learning for the quarter; develop and distribute one to two Tools or Resources that support the Sales Methodology, the Sales Process, or capability/skill building. • Review individual assessment data to identify high-performing salespeople who score well in the five personal leadership dimensions. • Meet with these individuals to understand career ambitions and establish a pipeline of people to consider for promotion.

Communicate	• Repeat and reinforce the illustrative Sales Vision. • Visually communicate by including posters and other collateral featuring the Sales Methodology and Sales Process. • Share highlights of development classes and resources that are planned for the year (SDP).	• Connect the Live Learning session to team assessment data and communicate the why behind any skills or dimensions that are the focus of the learning. • Promote and connect the dots between any Self-Paced Learning offered and the salesperson's work.	• Continue communicating the why and connecting the dots for salespeople around quarterly learning. • Ahead of assessing salespeople for a second time, position that this is to inform next year's investment in learning.	• Continue communicating the why and connecting the dots for salespeople around quarterly learning. • Encourage managers to share the company's intention to promote from within and the importance of deepening personal leadership capabilities.

LOOKING AHEAD

After two years, you can likely shift the focus toward fine-tuning efforts. Continued use of assessment data will show where your salespeople are strong capability-wise and where there are opportunities to keep investing. Fine-tuning will also guide future investments. Whether it is about bringing in specialized resources to address new initiatives in the Sales Development Plan or perhaps a technology buy to help salespeople accelerate results around a particular part of your Sales Methodology and Process, each of these decisions will be better informed and have a much better chance of succeeding.

Of course the bottom line is this: Taking on this plan-based Sales Effectiveness work is the only way to eliminate the dysfunctional cycle of "Ready, fire, aim!" that so many growth companies fall into and the troublesome inconsistency that comes with it. The Sales Effectiveness Program works because it mandates leadership buy-in. It requires alignment between the sales organization and the overall vision for the business. Finally, it addresses inconsistency in the function and among salespeople by implementing a shared framework and common language. This new cycle of buy-in, alignment, and common language now flows through each pillar of the Sales Effectiveness Program, including the establishment and sustainment of the Sales Methodology, Sales Process, and Sales Development Plan. Regular manager coaching that reinforces these elements within the context of everyday work creates stickiness and ensures staying power. But perhaps the crown jewel in all this remains the Diligence Framework and its ten dimensions. As salespeople grow in these capabilities, both from a core sales perspective and as individual leaders, they will be equipped to win in today's complex marketplace and be better positioned than the competition to take on the extraordinary changes on the horizon. Finally, this intentional, continual investment in your sales talent will also create an emotional connection to your organization that drives the discretionary effort required to reach higher levels of growth and scale.

About the Author

Specializing in sales performance improvement, Dayna Williams has developed award winning training content to serve hundreds of companies and thousands of salespeople over the last 20 years. She is currently leveraging those trends and insights to help venture backed firms build capable and efficient sales organizations that are ready to drive revenue growth and scale. Dayna has also co-created the Association for Talent Development's annual SELL conference and continues to support its broader sales enablement programming strategy.

Printed in Great Britain
by Amazon

43755150R00116